RETURN TO SEX
&
Intimacy

For Cancer Survivors
and Their Partners

MICHAEL J. RUSSER & JACQUELINE V. LOPEZ

SOS Institute
1187 Coast Village Rd.
Suite 1-193
Montecito, CA 93108
contact@SOSInstitute.org • 805-699-5504

ISBN: 978-0692886397

Cover designed by Lasso Design
Text design and typography by Lasso Design

Dedication:
This Book is for You

This book is for adult cancer survivors and their life partners, to help them regain and grow a deep sense of connection and intimacy in the face of the disease. Cancer is a shattering interruption to their daily lives, and especially to their most important and intimate relationships. It can devastate even the most loving of couples.

Ironically, the tragedy of cancer can also become the gateway to extraordinary levels of all forms of intimacy. Even greater than *before* the diagnosis. It is possible to transform the challenge of cancer into a life-affirming triumph, allowing one to become more connected to those around them—which vastly improves the expression of sex and intimacy.

We know firsthand this possibility. One of us (Michael), is a survivor of two forms of cancer that are still active. His treatments left him impotent. Jacqueline is Michael's post-menopausal life partner. Without her adventurous spirit, love and support, there would be nothing to share.

We are part of your community. We have similar challenges, doubts, anxieties, setbacks and uncertainties that are all part of having cancer as an unwelcome traveling companion on this adventure called Life. However, we found powerful ways to transcend and transform these challenges into a shared experience of such exquisite intimacy and sexual expression, it continues to boggle our minds.

This book is not an academic treatise written by individuals who may only clinically understand the disease and its implications. We wrote this book with firsthand, personal experience as our guide. It allowed us to compile our journeys, observations and insights. It helps us share how we, and other couples like us, have achieved incredible heights of sexual intimacy which most people (including doctors) thought impossible. By codifying what we did to achieve these extraordinary experiences, we feel confident you will see a clear, attainable path to transform your emotional and sexual intimacy.

This book is for you if you have or have had cancer, or are a partner of a cancer survivor. This book is for you, regardless of your religious or cultural background. It is for *any* couple seeking transformative intimacy. As you will see, the only requirements for experiencing deep, connecting intimacy, is a Heart[1] that is not afraid to give and receive love unconditionally, and a willingness to explore new ways of achieving that connection. Just know, we understand cancer's impact on relationships and are with you every step of the way. With that, we dedicate our work, and this book of intimate hope and possibility, to you.

---

1   Throughout this book you will notice, we always refer to 'heart' as Heart. That's because we live by the very empowering worldview that our Heart (metaphorically) is the true essence of who we are, and our ego is the false self. Our use of the capitalized form reflects this. This context, and the reasoning behind its use, is covered extensively within.

CONTENTS

Two Voices, One Story

You will find two, very distinct voices penned within these pages: mine and Jacqueline's. To help visually differentiate our unique perspectives, Jacqueline's contributions are set off by gray swashes on the left side of the page. For example…

Hi, this is Jacqueline, and I am deeply honored to offer my female perspective about sex and intimacy as Michael's life partner. Partners of cancer survivors are often affected just as much as their mates. I, like all of you, must contend with real and ongoing fears of losing my life partner, which I often do in silence.

Like many women in similar situations, I have been blessed to experience a natural transition to intimacy and sex outside the coital imperative. I have experienced a deep awakening away from a phallocentric model of sex. I learned to enjoy many ways of being intimate that would stay undiscovered if things for Michael were functioning 'properly.'

Prostate cancer invited me to stop and reflect on my priorities. Yes, cancer is a tough teacher, but with the love and support of all of our friends, family, and the people with whom we shared our experience, we were never alone. Throughout the book, we will present both of our perspectives surrounding aspects of our intimacy and relationship. I truly hope you will find added value in my contribution to this work.

Please keep in mind, this book is a detailed account of our experiences and the insights they generated. Although we stand behind the validity of our methods, we are not suggesting that our way is 'the' way. What we present here may not be for you. However, we discovered very empowering contexts, principles and insights that have consistently worked for us and others. Therefore, they will likely work for you in your quest to achieve intimate fulfillment, despite the challenges of cancer.

We believe any wisdom you glean from these pages is already inside you, just waiting to reveal itself. You will discover it is unnecessary to 'add' anything to increase your mutual experience of intimacy. The only requirement to enjoy the profound intimacy we share (and you deserve), is a willingness to let go of limiting beliefs and behaviors.

If you are in a committed relationship, we recommend that you and your partner each approach this material on your own individual terms. We have found that there are significant gender differences concerning the meaning and expression of intimacy. This book aims to provide an opportunity for an authentic, vulnerable and Heart-open discussion.

This book is for *all* cancer survivors looking to achieve deep intimacy with their partner, irrespective of the type of cancer that has affected their lives. For example, breast or ovarian cancer survivors and their partners will get just as much out of this book as those couples whose challenges with cancer are like ours. For survivors who are single, this book can prepare you for when you do enter into a committed relationship.

Lastly, even though our experience of intimacy is from a heterosexual perspective, the principals are universal. Throughout our journey, more than ever, we see that every human being seeks to connect with others at the Heart level—which goes beyond distinctions of race, creed, nationality, politics or gender identity. Our Hearts love all, unconditionally.

Glossary

In *Return to Sex and Intimacy*, Jacqueline and I use terms whose assigned meanings are often different from their standard or colloquial definitions. We offer this glossary for your reference to better understand the many new contexts presented. We encourage you to consider them as a more empowering way to view the complexities of human intimacy.

Authenticity – the willingness to show up without pretense or airs and always communicate (verbally or otherwise) your truth.

Awareness – a state of full-waking consciousness devoid of distraction, thought or emotion, allowing for the purest form of observation (see Observer).

BDSM – an acronym for Bondage, Domination, Sadism and Masochism typically conducted using a variety of often erotic practices, including role playing.

Captain Crunch and Munch Syndrome – the tendency of men to be overly aggressive when performing cunnilingus; often caused by the false assumption that this is what a woman wants or needs to climax.

Charge – an ego-based negative emotional reaction to an undesirable interaction or circumstance, often felt physiologically somewhere within the body.

Chemical Castration – a medical protocol designed to lower a man's testosterone level to near zero to starve his prostate cancer, which uses testosterone as its 'fuel.'

Connection – an unimpeded and unconditional sharing from the Heart between two human beings.

Conscious – a state of awareness outside the ego or voice in one's head.

Context – a paradigm that reflects one's worldview on some subset of reality.

Creating a Space – an unconditional invitation to connect via the Heart by an individual to one or more others.

Cucarachas – (Spanish for cockroach) the imaginary objectification of fear so it can be 'crushed' when it first shows itself or is felt.

Distinction – a specific meaning for a word or phrase that is often different or distinct from more typically used meanings.

Distraction – a state of fragmented awareness centered in the ego as it constantly looks for and craves new information, typically to avoid being fully present in the moment.

Ecstasy – a state of absolute bliss.

Ego – the false sense of self or separate identity typically associated with the voice within one's mind.

Ego vs. Heart – a context that views the true essence of a human being as their Heart not their ego.

Emotional Intimacy – a deep, abiding connection and emotional warmth between two human beings that may or not include sensual feelings.

Energetic – a condition or experience due to the free-flowing exchange or blockage of life-force energy.

Extraordinary Intimacy – emotional, sexual and spiritual intimacy that greatly exceeds the experience of most intimate couples.

Extraordinary Sexual Intimacy – sexual intimacy that consistently and substantially exceeds the experience of most intimate couples.

Feminine Sexual Energy – sexual energy biased toward passive receiving.

Full Body Orgasm – an uncontrolled physiological reaction or convulsing felt throughout the body because of a rapid buildup of life-force energy that may or may not include sexual arousal.

Gender Energy Swapping – the spontaneous switching of gender sexual energy expression between partners when making love.

Goalless Lovemaking – making love without goals, agendas or expectations of any outcome.

Heart – the immortal essence of who we are as human beings—an essence that gives and receives love continuously and unconditionally.

Intimacy – a deep, abiding connection between two people that can occur on the emotional, sexual and spiritual levels.

Isness – a condition or the way a circumstance simply is without creating a story around it.

Kundalini[2] – a form of primal energy located at the base of the spine… in physical terms, one commonly reports the Kundalini experience to be a feeling of electric current running along the spine.

---

2 https://en.wikipedia.org/wiki/Kundalini

LGBTQIA – an acronym typically used to address and identify the major non-heterosexual orientations including: Lesbian, Gay, Bi-sexual, Transsexual, Queer, Intersex and Asexual.

Libido – the innate drive for sexual release in the form of climax.

Life-force Energy – the force and energy that animates all living things and, within human beings, is closely related to sexual energy.

Making Love – an exchange of sexual energy between emotionally intimate individuals who are fully present for each other. It does not have to include penetrative sex.

Masculine Sexual Energy – sexual energy biased towards dominant giving.

Maslow's Hierarchy of Needs[3] – a theory in psychology proposed by Abraham Maslow in his 1943 paper *A Theory of Human Motivation* that essentially states that most individuals cannot focus on attaining higher level needs until their lower level ones are first met.

Monkey Mind – the condition of having one's mind driven by the ego into a constant state of distraction or turmoil.

Observer – one who is fully aware while observing without interaction or judgment, using most or all the physical and intuitive senses.

Open-Heartedness – the willingness to remove most, if not all, the barriers and protective armor put in place throughout one's life to avoid emotional pain.

---

3 https://en.wikipedia.org/wiki/Maslow%27s_hierarchy_of_needs

Orgasm – the sudden discharge of accumulated sexual excitement during the sexual response cycle, resulting in rhythmic muscular contractions in the pelvic region characterized by sexual pleasure.

Pain – an intense and unpleasant emotional and/or physical sensation (see Suffering).

Physical Intimacy – making love using direct physical contact that may include the genitals or not.

Presence – a state of full awareness in the present moment without distraction, agenda or judgment.

Reiki[4] – a form of alternative medicine developed in 1922 by Japanese Buddhist Mikao Usui that focuses on removing any blocks to the flow of life-force energy along the spinal column.

Relationship Failure – when either partner of a committed, intimate couple no longer feels fulfilled by the relationship, whether temporarily or permanently.

Relationship Life-cycle – a relationship model developed exclusively by the authors to identify and explain the six stages of most committed relationships.

Self-Actualization – the fulfillment of one's need to be fully alive and to find meaning in life, most often through selfless giving.

Sensuality – the condition of being pleasing or fulfilling to the senses.

Sex – genital contact between individuals for sexual arousal that may, but not necessarily, include intercourse.

---

4 https://en.wikipedia.org/wiki/Reiki

Sexual Arousal – increased sexual desire during, or in anticipation of, sexual activity.

Sexual Energy – the desire to express one's self sexually (closely related to life-force energy within humans).

Sexual Energy Continuum – a model of human sexuality developed by the authors which proposes that most individuals have both masculine and feminine sexual energy, regardless of their gender or orientation; it is a system that allows for subjective self-identification along a spectrum that traverses from 100% masculine to 100% feminine. *(A Continuum often explored within the LGBTQIA community to justify additional gender markers beyond the two binary markers of male and female.)*

Sexual Intimacy – making love using direct physical contact of the genitals that can include intercourse or not.

Sexual Life Force – life-force energy that is expressed and exchanged sexually.

Sexual Operating System (S.O.S) – an internally consistent advanced model of human intimate behavior developed exclusively by the authors.

Sexual Response Cycle[5] – a four-stage model of physiological response to sexual stimulation, which are, in order of occurrence: the excitement phase, plateau phase, orgasmic phase and resolution phase.
*The cycle was first proposed by William H. Masters and Virginia E. Johnson in their 1966 book **Human Sexual Response**.*

---

5 https://en.wikipedia.org/wiki/Human_sexual_response_cycle

Sexual Response Profile – the way an individual most effectively progresses through their sexual response cycle, which is typically different for men and women.

Sheeple – people who unconsciously follow the crowd or status quo because they are afraid to take responsibility for their own life experience.

Slash – denotes the gender infinite variation between male and female.

Space – an unspoken invitation from one person to another to join them in a state of full awareness and self-expression without judgment or expectations.

Spiritual Intimacy – the sharing of life-force energy between two people who already experience emotional intimacy.

Suffering – an ego-based attachment to pain or, resistance to 'what is'—typically used to support the notion or story of being a victim.

Surrender – letting go of resistance to 'what is.'

Tantra – the ancient Eastern religion art of enhancing and exchanging sexual and/or life-force energy between two people.

Transcendence – the experience of going beyond ego identification and experiencing oneness with everything (see Unity).

Transformation – the rapid shift of, often unconscious, beliefs that results in permanent changes of behavior and outcomes.

Unconscious – the state of being wherein one experiences life strictly from the perspective of one's ego.

Unity (or Spiritual Unity) – the temporary merging of life-force energy between two people, resulting in an, often temporary, loss of personal identity.

Vulnerability – a willingness to emotionally feel everything, including pain.

Introduction

I have learned that life is a lot like surfing, where we experience a series of never-ending 'waves': events ranging from pure ecstasy to pure horror. If you were anything like I was in my former life, you may have ignored them by becoming numb.

For most of my adult years I floated through life merely 'handling' my work, family and other obligations. That is, until two gigantic waves blindsided me. The first caused my 26-year marriage to end, and the second was the tsunami of cancer. I painfully realized, when we fight the waves of life, they always win, and they never care. They just *are*.

Skilled surfers know this. It is I who had to learn to embrace and harness their indomitable force for the best ride I could get. Ideally, without being pummeled.

I lost five members of my immediate family to cancer. The first one was my mother, who died of recurring breast cancer after a double radical mastectomy and struggling with the disease for years. My oldest sister underwent the same treatment progression with the same outcome. My oldest brother died of a rare blood cancer while my father succumbed to liver cancer. Most recently, another brother passed away due to melanoma that metastasized to his colon. In each case, their cancer was cruel. None of them, save my dad, lived past 70. At the time of this publication, I am 65.

Given my family's brutal history with cancer, my doctors have always kept a close eye for any sign of the beast. For years, regular annual checkups included frequent tests for colon and prostate cancer, which consistently returned negative results, until the Spring of 2011.

That is when my urologist noticed a slight up-tick in my PSA level, which was registering just over 2.0. He wasn't worried since my prostate was not enlarged and this was a relatively low level for a man of my age. However, just to be sure, he ordered another blood test for the following Fall. I thought so little of it, I don't even remember going in for it.

Shortly after that test, I received 'the call.' From the sound of my urologist's voice, I could tell something was wrong. This latest test showed my PSA had doubled to over 4.0 in just four months—not a good sign. After I hung up, I had this sinking feeling in the pit of my stomach; I was being hit by a large, unexpected wave.

In the subsequent biopsy, my urologist took 12 core samples of my prostate. The well-intentioned assurance of: *"You won't feel a thing..."* given before the procedure proved to be anything but true. A very distinctive 'ka-chaw' sound punctuated each sample taken, accompanied by a dull, clipping pain deep inside my pelvic region.

With the results that I now had the 'Big C', I made the immediate decision to have my prostate removed. Yes, I knew that the surgery could leave me impotent: yet another ominous wave that would have a profound impact on my intimacy for the rest of my now, potentially shortened life. I was vulnerable and scared, yet determined to defeat the disease that had decimated much of my family. I took all of five minutes to decide and tell my doctor: *"Take it out and take it out, now!"* After the surgery, my resulting impotence added a particularly ironic twist given my marriage ended just four months prior (a union in which the last 11 years were sexless by mutual agreement).

From these dramatic and tragic events, I learned many profound life lessons: insights I want to share with you and your partner to help spare your intimate relationship from the potential disruption of cancer.

Ironically, just two months before my diagnosis there was a major turning point in my life. I chose to no longer walk through life numbed, shutdown and obsessed about the next great achievement. Instead, I drew a line in the sand of my life and stepped over it from being a driven, disconnected individual to insisting on being *vulnerable* (willing to feel everything, including painful emotions), *authentic* (always saying my truth) and most importantly, *Heart-open* (removing most of the barriers I put over my Heart to 'protect' it from emotional wounding).

This transformation allowed my full humanity to emerge after a lifetime of hiding. I believe, with every fiber of my being, this shift has empowered Jacqueline and I to cope with my cancers and turn the worst nightmare of full clinical impotence into profound intimacy that neither she nor I had ever known or imagined.

While all cancers strive to destroy body, mind, and spirit, reproductive cancers can be even more devastating. The statistics are sobering. The American Cancer Society estimates that in 2016, the United States will see 246,260 new cases of breast cancer, 180,890 cases of prostate cancer, 22,280 cases of ovarian cancer and 8,720 cases of testicular cancer. Finally, according to the Prostate Cancer Foundation, between 40% and 70% of men who have surgery will experience erectile dysfunction.

When I expressed my concern about the impact seven weeks of intense, daily radiation would have on my already dwindling erectile function, my radiologist responded rather flippantly: *"Don't worry, we can fix anything!"* His apparent lack of empathy and understanding of the emotional impact of impending impotence left me rather cold and enraged.

Incidentally, the rampant lack of empathy and resources to help with cancer's impact on intimacy is the number one complaint of survivors and partners. It appears there is a systemic failure of the medical community to discuss these issues despite the overwhelming mayhem that cancer wreaks on couples everywhere.

To be fair, oncologists receive little training on sexuality or the emotional impacts of cancer and its treatment. They are under enormous pressure to cure the ever-increasing numbers of people diagnosed with cancer each year. These doctors suffer the subtle-yet-powerful emotional effects of working with patients who may not survive, despite their best efforts. This can take a huge personal toll given that 38% of oncologists report burnout according to a 2013 Medscape.com study. Even more telling, according to a landmark study by the Mayo Clinic, urologists have a 63.6% burnout rate, second only to emergency room personnel.[6]

With great respect, we know our doctors are doing incredible work saving our lives and helping us maintain quality of life. I wouldn't be here without them. We can't expect them to do everything perfectly throughout the complex and challenging process of mitigating cancer. This book, ideally, will also serve as their resource to help patients and partners successfully navigate cancer's impact to their relationship.

What you hold in your hands is our commitment to help you traverse the dark tunnel of fear, uncertainty and doubt. Consider it your guide to help you surf the waves of cancer and its impact to your intimate relationships. We have taken a holistic approach that promises to bring renewed intimacy back into your lives. All we ask is that you stay open to the well-documented possibilities presented.

It is our greatest hope that *Return to Sex and Intimacy* will serve as a catalyst to help you and your partner transform the tragedy of cancer into a triumph of deep love, intimacy and fulfilling sexual expression.

Passionately,

Michael J. Russer / Jacqueline V. Lopez

---

6 https://www.usnews.com/news/articles/2016-09-08/doctors-battle-burnout-to-save-themselves-and-their-patients

SECTION 1

Acceptance & Surrender

"*The best things in life are not those we make happen, but which are allowed to show up because we simply got out of the way.*"

~ ANONYMOUS

The phrase 'Fighting cancer' is common within our community of cancer survivors. It implies a willingness to do whatever it takes to beat a disease that seems determined to shorten our lives and impact their quality. Within this and other contexts, 'surrender' connotes a giving up, weakness and lack of resolve. Our culture views none of these kindly: an easy judgment from those who don't have to confront the beast.

However, when you combine surrender with acceptance of your current circumstances, you unleash an unstoppable force within you: a power that can propel you past the anger, frustration, and sense of victim-hood that can arise from the often-debilitating effects of this disease and its treatments.

We have found accepting and surrendering to the 'what is' of cancer's impact on our lives is the threshold to transcending our perceived limitations—especially those concerning sex and intimacy. The chapters within this section help you free up whatever energy you may have put towards resisting the impact of your cancer, whether surgical scarring, impotence, chemotherapy et cetera... Most of these techniques work for many of life's other challenges. Think of it as preparing the soil for life-affirming intimacy that will blossom as it basks in the warmth and glow of your open Heart.

Acceptance and surrender are the greatest blessings you can give yourself as you begin this new and exciting journey toward deep, fulfilling intimacy that no cancer can touch.

Chapter 1

THE FINE ART OF SURRENDER

Rage

The first phase of dealing with this diagnosis was realizing I was facing major issues about ever having a normal erection again. My timid hope dissolved into disbelief, then a seething rage. I remember times looking up at the ceiling, shaking my fists to the heavens, shouting to whatever Higher Power would listen: *"You have GOT to be f***ing kidding me!!!!!!"* As if it were God's fault for my predicament while giving me no credit whatsoever for remaining faithful to my sexless marriage.

Fortunately, for me, this period of victimhood was short lived. For many men, however, erectile dysfunction is considered 'worse than death.' The despair lies in the thinking that someone with erectile dysfunction is no longer 'a man'... this couldn't be further from the truth. Physical side-effects of cancer can never change who we are at our core.

Any reproductive cancer, in a male or a female, can have a tremendous negative impact on someone's sexual self-image. If you are a man facing treatment for prostate cancer, your thoughts, like mine, often include: What's it like to pee? Will I have incontinence and will it turn off my partner? Will I ever have an orgasm again? What will happen to my libido? What if my friends or associates find out I have erectile dysfunction? Will I still feel like a man? Will my partner stop finding me attractive?

This condition often has a profound impact on your partner as well. They may think you are no longer interested or attracted to them. Even though they understand they are not the cause, it still can be difficult to reconcile emotionally. Likewise, women going through the rigors of cancer and its treatment, particularly breast and other female reproductive cancers, can feel 'less than a woman' with the same concerns about their attractiveness.

If you or your partner are experiencing any of this, there are ways to transcend this sense of loss and diminishment. It is quite possible to reestablish, and even exceed, your previous experience of emotional and sexual intimacy. Whatever your circumstances, don't give up hope. Instead, we invite you to be open to the possibilities shared throughout this book. Consider them as a proven guide to an adventure you can share with your partner, leading to greater levels of intimacy and sexual fulfillment.

Thankfully, my mounting anger did not plunge me into deep depression or feelings of shame. I realized shame is a terribly destructive emotion, in which far too many men find themselves trapped; this is due to unfortunate cultural imprinting that equates manhood with a functioning penis. Once I was over anger, I moved on to 'bargaining'— which meant I would do whatever it took to get my erections back. Man, did I ever.

Besides the usual erectile aids, I tried much more powerful intraurethral and injectable medications, and even a penis pump. None of these were very effective, or in the case of the penis pump, particularly romantic. Once it was clear the usual medical treatments did little to help my situation, I considered more radical remedies such as surgical implants, which I decided against primarily for their post-surgical risks. After that, I explored unconventional therapies that just might do the trick. These non-traditional methods included Chinese herbal medications, Reiki energy work, meditation, massage, acupuncture, colon cleansing, Watsu water massage and even a Shaman (no, really!)

who beat a drum and danced around my prone body in a small, dark, incensed-filled room.

Nearly everyone from the medical community to the well-intentioned unorthodox practitioners were reassuring me my penis would soon have a modicum of normal erectile function. These encouraging notions helped me adopt a wait-and-see attitude. I was willing to wait because I wasn't seeing anyone. In fact, I had decided to move to Brazil for a few months to figure out what was next for me.

I will admit, however, I had fantasized about meeting a sensual Brazilian woman who might just nurse me back to reasonable intimate enjoyment. That's the one thing the doctors and other practitioners hadn't considered.

It is intriguing how life sometimes gives us exactly what we need and often, many times greater than what we wanted. I did meet a wonderful, sensuous Brazilian woman... but not in Brazil. I also never got my erectile function back. Meeting her showed me I didn't need it after all.

Instead, what I got was an incredible opening to ever-growing emotional, sexual and spiritual ecstasy, far exceeding what I ever believed possible. This was achieved without medication, 'toys' or aids of any kind. I can honestly say all of this occurred because of my full impotence, not despite it.

Ponder that last sentence carefully. As difficult as it may be to believe, this experience of elevated intimacy is also available for both of you.

Now it is time to introduce Jacqueline, my life partner and Intimacy Muse. I have the utmost confidence that you will see what an amazing, courageous woman she is. She is my inspiration and the inspiration for this book.

I am Jacqueline Lopez

 I still wonder, did it really happen? Did I find the most exquisite intimacy with a man who can't get it up to save his life? For 10 years I was previously in a committed relationship. Two years after becoming single again, when I least expected it, I met Michael. My friend and I were standing outside our local Unity Church, trying to figure out what to do next. I had mixed up the date for a particular talk that evening. Michael showed up for another talk about life transitions and asked us in which room it was being held. As he walked by us, I sniffed his scent. My friend who was with me, looked at me strangely trying to understand my reaction. I composed myself but the next words out of my mouth were: *"Hmm... Did you smell him?"* My friend paid little attention. But I couldn't let him go. I immediately suggested we check out the talk where this gentleman was heading. We followed him and I sat three seats away. After the talk, we connected and became friends which eventually led to us dating. After that, we continued dating for four years before we moved in together. I mention our timeline because it's important to show we took the time necessary for a solid relationship to 'take root' and grow strong. Ours has grown like a redwood tree. We can weather any storm.

At this point in my life, I realize that what I want in a partner is someone open to exploring unconventional ways to be intimate. I am a 51-year-old raised by a single mother, the oldest of three siblings raised in South America. I am here sharing the most intimate details of my life with you so Michael and I can help couples struggling with cancer-related intimacy challenges. You will see I am not your average South American woman.

My mother had an enormous influence on who I am today. She believed in raising us 'free-range' in terms of education. She never tried to persuade us to go to college or to pursue specific careers. We weren't even a highly religious family, despite being raised in a Catholic culture. Her strong independence instilled confidence in each of us to act on the things in our best interest.

My parents married young; my mother was 19 and my father

21. My father came from a traditional paternalistic family. Not only do such men deeply believe their superiority over women, the women in my culture sustain that belief. However, my mother is inherently strong and always believed something beyond herself was guiding her to do the things she did to thrive in a male-dominated society. She was my inspiration and absolute hero. However, to show how insidious social programming is, she too, fell prey to patriarchy while she raised two girls and a boy.

Although there were few demands on me, there was one thing my mother expected, since I was the last to live at home after graduating from college: that I would get married and have children. In our culture, girls leave home only after finding a suitable husband. There were no other options.

Despite that, I did it differently. Once I saved enough money for a down payment, I moved into my own apartment. In doing so, I savored freedom for the first time and it was delicious.

I never had a strong desire to follow what my friends were doing, which meant not following the script imposed by parents, the educational system or society. They expected me, along with all women my age, to 'do the right thing.' My 'right thing' was doing what was best for me.

I don't know who made this list of milestones for girls. They always seemed like rules. The adulthood template looks something like this: having a career path, being married or coupled before 25, having a kid, owning a home and so on. I realized meeting these milestones weren't interesting.

The question was, how do you figure out what it means to be an adult if you haven't achieved those milestones? During a speech at Stanford University, Oprah Winfrey said something that spoke to me: *"If you have no idea what your purpose is, don't panic, the key is to know what you don't want to be or do. Then, identify them and stay away from them! Your purpose will show up later."*

When I turned thirty and still hadn't found my purpose or 'The One', my mother worried I'd end up alone with nobody to take care of me when I grew old. Or worse, I would never have children. That makes me laugh because during my teenage years, she threatened to show me the door and disown me if I ever became pregnant out of wedlock. Now, she was backpedaling, begging me to have at least one child or else a pervasive darkness would forever cloud my life, because I didn't fulfill the ultimate female mission.

However, the more I exposed myself to new ideas through reading and meeting influential people, achieving my ultimate fulfillment as a wife and mother seemed too limiting. I sensed there was, and eventually discovered, a wonderful limitless world waiting for me to explore. The more I read and the more people I met, the more my feelings about love and intimacy changed. I realized the disturbing things I had learned started with the slanted story of Adam and Eve in the Garden of Eden.

I believe the Creation Story to be the most catastrophic PR campaign against women and sexuality ever known. From my perspective it was a team effort by the Judeo-Christian tradition to spread guilt, and the omnipresent fear of hell, both of which make our lives hellish.

Fast forward. Now, as a post-menopausal woman, I no longer have the slightest guilt about my lifestyle and, most importantly, about my sexual fulfillment, which has shifted gradually over the years. Changes in female sexual desire are more about *how* women want to experience sex, not *if* they want it. We do!

As women, we still have a long way to go to claw our way out of the Victorian, guilt-ridden society in which we live. This guilt seems to have sown the seeds of many erroneous assumptions that can easily trip us up, even within the most compatible relationships. I think Michael feels lucky we don't have to combat those issues at this stage in our lives.

Many women assume men know what women want sexually, but they really don't. Many men hope their partner will remain unchanged, seeking the same form of intimacy as they did when they first met many years ago. Often, they don't. I, too, fell prey to these same assumptions. I wasn't even aware of them until I realized I wasn't getting them. That's until I became a more conscious person, I met Michael and we started on this journey together to find a whole new level of emotional and sexual fulfillment.

During my childbearing years, I admit, I used to find traditional sexual intercourse very appealing. This was due to my innate wiring, intended for procreation and survival of the species. Later, like many other women, as I approached my 40s, the ticking of my biological clock grew louder. For me, this was a minor annoyance, but for others, it's a strident reminder of their primary purpose (biologically speaking), which is to bear offspring—ideally with a man who will adequately support and protect the family. This physiological reminder, along with well-intentioned pressure from family and friends, often causes women to make poor choices they come to regret. However, I have learned from every relationship I've ever had. Each one was part of the journey of realizing who I am.

The second realization I had came from understanding the impact of the cultural and religious beliefs around female sexuality. In Western culture, sexuality is often deeply rooted in shame and ignorance. Upon arriving in the United States for the first time, it quickly became apparent that the word sex has a significant charge. The United States is probably one of the most uptight countries in the world regarding human sexuality. There seems to be an intangible barrier most people never cross when talking about it. That's why men and women grow up with so much guilt-driven anxiety and repression of their own desires.

If nothing else, learn about your sexual self for survival reasons. If women know little about their own anatomy, it could cost them their lives. According to a new survey in the UK done by the gynecological cancer charity The Eve Appeal, 44% of women could not identify the vagina and 60% were unsure where the vulva was.

In Latin countries, discussion about sex is no more charged than talking about the weather. For us, sex is natural and not considered immoral or dirty. I realized avoiding the discussing of sex openly and authentically has caused many Western women to experience tremendous shame about their bodies and because of that, never understand their full sensual potential.

When my niece was a teenager and dating her boyfriend, my sister always asked her boyfriend if he wanted condoms. In my country, it's common for parents to ask their daughter's boyfriend whether he needs condoms for the night. I think that is a great example of parents being honest, realistic and encouraging about the inevitability of this natural phenomenon called sex. This is a great example of a responsible culture that takes preventative measures to avoid potentially disastrous outcomes.

I noticed a stark difference between living in South America and in the U.S. There's a strong cultural message to women in most developed countries to pursue success in a world designed for men, and to compete tooth-and-nail for their place in the corporate arena. The fast-moving modern world means women are working longer hours, juggling more responsibilities, and progressively less able to place their intimate relationship as their top priority. In my humble opinion, this frantic rush for success which has permeated femininity has done great collateral damage to the balance of the masculine and feminine.

Most men in South America are 'machista' which means they believe in an exaggerated sense of manliness and dominance over women. Pursuing gender parity at a slower pace found in South America helps balance male and female roles. This is opposite to the clash I see happening to couples in Western societies.

I fully support every woman who pursues breaking glass ceilings in her career, however, I encourage her to take off the 'corporate cape' when she returns home from the trenches. At home you are his woman and he is your man. Your mate longs for the alluring soft, sweet and sexy feminine side of you. When you walk through that door, take a deep breath and shake out all traces of dominance that rubbed off in the boardroom battles you had to contend with that day. Don't forget that your man has also had to deal with dominant behavior from the other men in his office. When both of you take it down a notch, you will enjoy just being yourselves together.

My perspective may sound antiquated for one who claims to be a modern woman. However, I feel I represent a more balanced view of femininity that works effectively when joined with a man's perspective of himself. My views definitely changed as I aged. It has taken time for me to no longer have the urge to please a man to keep him. Now my focus is on keeping my myself intact as a woman. Age has freed me to be myself which includes knowing and embracing the full spectrum of my sexuality. Along with that, I am now more vocal about what I want emotionally and sexually.

Fortunately, I met Michael, an emotionally evolved man, who relishes these traits in me. He receives his greatest sexual fulfillment by helping me achieve mine. I learned from Michael that there's nothing more satisfying to a man (who truly cares for you) than knowing he can please you, unlike any other. With that being said, my sexual desire for Michael grows stronger every day because its foundation is the deep and growing emotional connection we share.

Hopefully this helps you understand who I am and what Michael has in me as a woman and partner in his life's journey. To all women reading this, it's crucial you embrace and accept your sexuality and body as the beautiful and unlimited fountain of sensuality it truly is.

This book is an exploration into the incredible journey Michael and I share. A journey that continues with no end in sight. It is my hope for all the women and men reading this, that you find extraordinary intimacy which serves you both, physically, emotionally and spiritually.

We realize that you may be among the majority of readers who have been with a partner for many years before cancer knocked on your door. Nearly every long-term couple encounters emotional wounding that can inhibit access to the kinds of intimacy shown within this book. We are living proof that intimacy *can* grow stronger the longer you are together, even with the challenges of cancer.

Starting out slowly

Jacqueline and I met under the most unusual circumstances. I was preparing for my three-month trip to Brazil and was not particularly interested in starting a relationship with anyone before leaving. Jacqueline had just ended a marriage one year earlier and given up on dating.

While we found each other interesting, neither one of us fell head-over-heels. This ended up being a good thing because it was our first step of a shared journey towards extraordinary intimacy. This included developing a foundation of deep emotional intimacy and friendship before we even thought about becoming physical. This is an important consideration when in a committed relationship. You will find that re-establishing genuine emotional intimacy is *crucial* to experiencing fulfilling sexual intimacy, especially within the context of cancer.

For the next several weeks after we met, Jacqueline and I deepened our so-far platonic relationship. When she wasn't helping me find and negotiate a place to stay in Brazil or learn rudimentary Portuguese, we hiked together during the week and danced to live music on Friday nights at a local pub.

During the times we shared a dance floor, it became clear our friendship may blossom into something more. Of course, I was leaving for Brazil in just six weeks: hardly ideal conditions to start a new relationship.

One night, we sat in the car chatting after driving back from one of our Friday evening dance dates. Without warning or much thinking, I impulsively reached over and gave her a quick kiss on the lips, just a peck. She was the first woman I had kissed besides my ex-wife in well over 30 years. The stunned look on Jacqueline's face practically shouted: *"Uh, oh..."* The fact that my face wasn't slapped, and that no awkward dialog ensued, fueled my otherwise wobbly confidence.

A couple of days later, as she was leaving my apartment, I kissed her again, a little more ardently this time. It was at that moment our eyes met and silently revealed where things were heading. The only problem: I still hadn't mentioned my 'condition'—something I was not looking forward to sharing, yet clearly necessary.

We agreed to meet the following Saturday afternoon at my place to discuss what might happen next. Keep in mind, initially neither one of us found the other overly attractive. So, imagine my surprise when I opened the door and standing before me was a woman who almost took my breath away.

As she gracefully walked over to my couch to take a seat, my fear-machine was working overtime. How would she react when I tell her I can't get it up to save my life? Would she glance at her watch and say: *"My, will you look at the time? I have to go now but we'll be in touch, b-bye!"* Or give me a look that said: *"You poor guy..."* which would be a sting of unwanted sympathy causing the further deflation of my self-image as a man. I didn't know what to expect.

I took my place next to her on the couch and looked into her beautiful eyes, reflecting the afternoon sunlight streaming in from the window. This was the moment of truth. As I pointed to my crotch I said: *"Sweetie, this isn't working and it may never work. Are you willing to explore other ways of being intimate with me?"* Though I said the words, I was clueless as to what that could entail.

She replied without a hint of hesitation: *"Sure!"* All those angst-ridden hours of anticipatory anxiety and she says, *"Sure!"* Upon hearing it, my Heart leapt for joy. With Jacqueline's unexpected reassurance, we immediately planned our first intimate encounter. We reserved a suite the following Saturday at a private and romantic hot springs resort about 100 miles north of Santa Barbara, California. I could barely wait.

At this point in my journey, I hadn't given up performing like a 'normal' man. So, I brought the full contingent of erectile aids that money can buy including the highest dose of Cialis® one can purchase. A potent intraurethral drug called Muse®, which is so powerful that if any normally functioning man were foolish enough to try it, he *would* go to the hospital four hours later for relief, if you know what I mean. Just in case those drugs didn't work as advertised, I brought the 'failsafe', the penis pump. I was locked, loaded and ready to go.

Or, so I thought...

After taking the Cialis® upon arrival, Jacqueline and I took a soothing soak in the hot tub to give it time to work. Then we proceeded to the bed where we engaged in wonderfully gentle foreplay. It had been over 12 years without sex and here I was naked with the most beautiful, sensuous, wonderful woman I'd ever met. To say I was excited is the world's greatest understatement. However, my excitement wasn't showing where it needed to most.

After almost an hour of continued foreplay it was clear to both of us the Cialis® wasn't working. So, I suggested that we move to the big guns and try the Muse®. To her credit, she helped me insert the self-dissolving Muse capsule into my urethra, neither a pleasant nor particularly sexy process. Yet we were good-natured about it and laughed at the absurdity of it all. After another 20 minutes of sensuous foreplay… nothing, nada, zip. At that point, I wasn't laughing anymore and experienced the first pangs of deep performance anxiety.

As little beads of sweat formed on my forehead, I issued a silent prayer: *"Please God, don't let me down, not now!"* With as much of a reassuring smile as I could muster, I turned to Jacqueline and said: *"Sweetie, no problem, I brought the penis pump, and it HAS to work because it's based on physics!"* Meanwhile she's lying on her side with a pinched look that silently said: *"Are we going to do this every time we make love?"* With somewhat renewed confidence and absolute determination, I pumped for all I was worth. At first, I saw and felt results, *"Finally! Thank God!"* That is, until at the height of my pumping frenzy, I suddenly keeled over in excruciating, eye-bulging pain… having just sucked in my left testicle. Sweat was now pouring down my face in rivulets as I sat on the edge of the bed, shoulders hunched over in total, abject despair. The voice in my head cruelly whispered: *"It's over. It's over before it even started."*

Then, at this lowest point of my life, something profoundly deep and unexpected happened. That voice in my head went silent with the complete acceptance of my impotence. I surrendered. I fully embraced the 'is-ness' of my circumstances, no longer having any urge to fight or overcompensate for it. Quietly, I turned to Jacqueline, looked deep into her large brown eyes and said: *"I'm done. I'm done with all of this. Let's just lay together and see what happens."*

We made exquisite love, the likes of which neither of us had previously experienced. Our lovemaking began late afternoon and didn't finish until almost midnight. We blew right through dinner and had nothing substantive to eat due to five or six straight hours of lovemaking. We had to force ourselves to go to sleep because we ended up having more energy after we finished than when we began. Upon waking, we skipped breakfast and made love again for hours, until it was time to check out.

Shortly after this experience, Jacqueline and I discussed what happened and how astounding it was. Thanks to that inquiry, we came to several new and surprising insights about what intimacy actually means. The first thing we realized is the word 'performance' has no business in the bedroom—*ever*. Instead, we replaced it with *Presence*. Which means being in the moment, in a state of full awareness, without distractions, goals or expectations. This alone allowed us to enjoy levels of intimacy we suspect most couples would give anything for if they only knew it existed.

My biggest 'Aha!' was: how a man defines himself is a choice. It can be based on the size and capability of his 'package', as popular culture and pharmaceutical companies would have us believe, or how deeply he connects with and pleases his partner in the way they want. This realization has tremendously empowering implications for any man or woman impacted by impaired bodily function or body shame, regardless of the cause. Any of my lingering shame or self-consciousness surrounding my impotence had completely evaporated. After that first intimate experience with Jacqueline, I never felt more like a man. My inability to release or climax during this first experience in over 12 years didn't bother me one bit. In fact, I had never in my life known such fulfillment.

At this point, you might wonder how we achieved these exquisite and prolonged heights of sexual satisfaction despite my clinical impotence and our refusal to use any aids. Please trust we will reveal all in the following chapters.

Off to Brazil

Just a few short weeks later, the departure for my life-reset trip to Florianopolis, Brazil, which would be my home for the next three months, was fast approaching. I had given up my apartment, so as much as I didn't want to leave Jacqueline, I needed to follow through with my plan.

Once settled into my new South American environment, we saw each other daily via online video, which had me longing for her even more. After being there just two weeks I realized I did not want to spend Christmas without her. Around mid-December I flew back and rented a funky little room in a quirky home where we could stay together until I returned to Brazil right after New Year's. Those two weeks together were amazing. The awful weather in Santa Barbara did not prevent us from having the most incredible time together in that small room, making love for untold hours day after day. It was our honeymoon period. The levels of emotional and physical intimacy we experienced made our first encounter at the hot-springs resort seem almost uneventful.

I often wondered, *how is it possible that it keeps getting better and better?* I even grew anxious, pondering what would it be like when I returned from Brazil for good. As you will see, those fears were unfounded. In fact, at the time of this writing, our current depth and expression of all forms of intimacy makes our Christmas honeymoon, nearly five years ago, pale in comparison.

Upon returning to the beautiful beaches of Brazil, I walked aimlessly while pondering what our extraordinary Christmas together meant. We had stumbled upon powerful and unique ways to help ourselves and countless other couples struggling with cancer-related intimacy issues. I remember being quite excited, with a newfound sense of purpose for this next phase of my life.

I reached out to several prostate cancer support groups to interview other survivors and partners from around the world. By the time I returned to Santa Barbara and into Jacqueline's arms, I was on a mission.

Great surrender

Thanks to this first intimate adventure, I have discovered another side to surrender, one far more empowering and transformative than the greatest feats of heroism. Opening yourself up to this shift in how you view and use surrender means living a life full of self-expression and unimagined possibilities instead of one based on fear and frustration.

Not giving up, accepting

While 'giving up' implies resignation and a sense of powerlessness, acceptance of 'what is' opens the door to possibilities. Acceptance empowers without giving anything away. When you accept what is, you are no longer struggling with the 'isness', which frees you up to explore, discover and experience other wonders that await.

Here's what I discovered through this whole process: to accept what is, is equivalent to surrendering to the possibility of transformation. Once I stopped fighting and resisting what *was*, vast new worlds of intimate experiences and insights became available to both Jacqueline and I.

There is a strong cultural imprint in our society implying that we must do whatever it takes to achieve a certain end, and anything short of that is defeat. In what I have shared, it should be clear that my acceptance and surrender was anything but a sign of weakness. Without it, I would have remained a very frustrated, angry man.

If you find you are still resisting your current circumstances due to cancer, or any of life's other challenges, consider that surrendering to their isness can be your most courageous act towards intimate healing; it opens yourself and your partner to the extraordinary experiences described within the pages that follow.

Chapter 2

A BETTER MAN

The ManKind Project

During the year between my first cancer diagnosis and meeting Jacqueline, I was on an epic journey of self-discovery. This meant I was saying 'Yes!' to many new experiences, perhaps subconsciously knowing I had so much more to learn about myself and my inherent limiting beliefs before I would ever be ready for a lasting relationship.

One day I was sharing with a female acquaintance of mine how I felt uncomfortable around most men. I told her I didn't trust them and because of that, had developed no real male friends. She mentioned her husband belonged to a group called The ManKind Project, and that they had a three-day weekend course called the New Warrior Training Adventure (NWTA). She suggested I attend the next one to help resolve my long-simmering issues with men dating back to my father and three older brothers: my dominant family members who made it abundantly clear I was not a 'real man.'

So, with little added consideration, I signed up for the weekend that was three months away in September of 2012. For those ensuing three months, I didn't give it much thought as I was busy planning my extended life-reset trip to Brazil. I was also winding down a volatile business relationship with a former friend. When the day came to drive to the retreat location where the NWTA was being held, I was experiencing extreme anxiety about the possibility of having to sue this person. I showed up in the middle of nowhere on a late Friday afternoon, distraught, not wanting to be there and not knowing what to expect.

The interesting thing about saying 'Yes!' to things you don't fully understand, is it's difficult to find excuses to not follow through. After arrival, I soon forgot my troubles and became wholly immersed in this new experience.

The NWTA is a powerful transformational training designed for men to address their deepest fears and blocks in life within a safe space. The program helps men become confident, whole and able to embrace all aspects of their masculinity with an open Heart while retaining their sense of manhood.

Over 60,000 men worldwide have completed the NWTA over the last 30 years, driven mostly by word-of-mouth. What each man gets out of their experience is unique for them. The biggest impact this weekend had for me, was releasing the pent-up rage I still had for my father, who had passed away from cancer 25 years prior. He was an emotionally stunted authoritarian who used brute force to get his point across. I had no idea how much I truly hated aspects of him until it showed up that weekend.

One exercise in particular, allowed me to express fully my deeply buried anger. At one point, it took six men, each much larger than me, to hold me back from tearing limb-from-limb a stand-in I chose to represent my father and his total dominance. Once I could manifest that rage and release it, I compassionately and tearfully forgave my dad. In that moment, my relationship with men transformed *completely*. After that, I could trust, engage and form deep bonds with men without hesitation. I had learned to genuinely enjoy their company.

Another interesting thing happened during that weekend reminded me of my sorry state of full impotence, in an almost comical way. The facilitators directed attendees to break into small groups to discuss sex, sexuality, and intimacy. *Oh, swell!*

As we passed around a massive wooden phallus to indicate our turn to share, I couldn't have felt more inadequate. Here's this ridiculously large reminder of what may never be again! To add a final dash of salt to my wounds, one man in our group shared how he and his wife now experience two-hour love-making sessions.

Besides my extreme disbelief, shared I'm sure, by the others in our small circle—all I could think as he spoke was: *"Really?!"* Little did I know, his declarations of extended love-making foretold my very near future.

This weekend experience couldn't have been better timed. I met Jacqueline just two weeks later. If I hadn't reconciled and healed my rage, I doubt we would have lasted as a couple.

A better man, a better lover

It turns out my erectile dysfunction gave me the opportunity to slow down as a lover and focus on my partner, Jacqueline, instead of taking care of my hard-on, as I had always previously done.

Research has shown, time and time again, most women's intimate encounters are not satisfying, despite what male egos tell us. Regarding penetrative sex, just about the time most men issue their last grunt and roll over, their partner is just getting warmed-up.

Thanks to my erectile dysfunction, making love has become an exquisite process, not a goal. My E.D. has allowed me to match my partner's sexual response profile so closely, we each have wonderful intimate experiences, *every time*. Our new normal is multi-hour love-making sessions with Jacqueline typically climaxing many times.

In case you suspect she must be some sort of sex goddess, think again. She is a post-menopausal woman who never experienced sex like this. Keep in mind, all of this happens with me being 100% flaccid and using no auxiliary aids.

Talk about it

Impotence is not only something most men aren't willing to discuss, but it's something they aren't willing to hear others share. The way some men react, you'd think impotence was contagious. I remember a time Jacqueline and I were at an outdoor church luncheon. At our table was a woman in her 50s and a man in his mid-40s. As small talk turned into: *"So, what do you do?"* I shared the story of how my E.D. was the biggest blessing to our relationship and why. The woman got it instantly. This is typical of the reaction we receive from most women with whom we share our story. Our male guest however, had a look of shock and incredulity as he subtly backed his chair away from the table, finally blurting out: *"Well, that will never happen to me!"* Bless her Heart, Jacqueline didn't miss a beat when she responded with: *"I hope it never comes back."*

Truth is, erectile dysfunction *is* the best thing that has ever happened to our intimate life.

There, I said it.

I say it a lot during speeches, on the radio, on TV, in print, online and occasionally at large gatherings (it's a great way to quiet a room down if things get rowdy).

My impotence has been a powerful context and gateway to discovering the true meaning of intimacy, something I never would have known otherwise. This is not about me showing off my sexual metamorphosis. Instead, it is about my Heart opening, which was a crucial step for me to turn the tragedy of cancer-induced impotence into the triumph of sublime intimacy. I will now turn this over to Jacqueline, so she can share her story of how I became a better man in loving her.

> When I met Michael in my late forties, I was at the tail end of menopause, and on a journey to become a more conscious human being. I had the 'soil prepped' for this upcoming chapter in my life. Though happy being single, I longed to give and receive love unconditionally with a suitable mate. Many women quit looking because it's exhausting. If you find someone, keeping a

relationship together is complex, and in most cases, not worth the effort.

I hesitated to date Michael because he appeared to be heading to a destination he had not yet identified. Nevertheless, I found his kindness, intelligence, uncanny humor and scent, very attractive.

When Michael broke the news by pointing to his crotch and saying, *"Sweetie, this is not working and it may never work,"* I put myself in his shoes and immediately had deep compassion for what he risked at that moment. I recognized the tremendous courage he had. The realization that his E.D. would not impede the new me and the wholeness of his spirit caused me to experience sheer joy. The adventurous side of me said, *"Wow! This is a unique opportunity to try something different."* I had no idea what that would look like, but I was excited! Now, after exploring these possibilities, I'm convinced that a menopausal woman's greatest wet dream is a man with erectile dysfunction.

Freud called the female sexuality the 'dark continent.' This underscored his theorizing that the center of female pleasure is the reproductive tract, and if it doesn't end in an orgasm, the cause is frigidity. Freud also said that clitoral orgasms are 'infantile.' Unfortunately, his views and 'dark continent' labeling was the platform for millions of fake orgasms around the world. By the mid-20th century, Alfred Kinsey's systematic studies redirected the center of female orgasm and sensitivity away from the vagina and back to where it belongs.

Our culture continues to discredit and dismiss women's sexual pleasure. This is true even in some quarters of the medical community including respected sources such as *Gray's Anatomy* by Dr. Henry Gray. Women can also be their own worst enemies concerning their sexual pleasure. Less than a third of the women surveyed in the UK gynecological study

I mentioned earlier in the book could correctly identify all six parts of their reproductive system.

For the edification of both genders, here are important clitoral facts:

♡ It's structure in its entirety (including internal parts) is fairly equal in size to an average non-erect penis.

♡ It has erectile tissue that swells when aroused.

♡ The clitoris has twice as many nerve endings as a penis.

♡ It's located outside the vagina.

♡ The clitoris can engorge continuously without a refractory period—allowing anyone with a healthy clitoris to experience multiple orgasms.

♡ Surprisingly, it is the only human organ that exists exclusively for pleasure.

I have heard many woman state: *"My partner couldn't find my clitoris if I drew a map!"* That made me reflect upon how many women could coach their mate to pleasure them if they themselves didn't know what's down there.

Instead of treating the vagina and clitoris as separate entities, consider them as an interconnected network of nerves and muscles. One variable is the type and location of physical stimulation during sex. Rather than label an orgasm as vaginal or clitoral, it makes more sense to think of orgasm in terms of the overall experience, including the emotional connection with your mate.

More often than not, many women fail to achieve orgasm even if their partner appears to be doing all the right things. A female climax involves the entire body, emotions, perceptions, memories, senses, and most importantly, time to warm up.

While knowledge of female sexuality is vital to a fulfilling heterosexual relationship, it requires more. The male partner must be coachable and willing to be adventurous, especially if he is dealing with cancer. Our relationship has only become stronger because Michael is a man that has not allowed shame of erectile dysfunction to diminish our sexual intimacy. If anything, by working together, he has turned this 'worst nightmare' into the biggest blessing for our intimacy.

Chapter 3

IMPOTENCE, MARRIAGE AND SEX

Shame—the relationship destroyer

A few years ago, a woman reached out to me to help her fiancé of two years cope with his impotence. When he discovered he could no longer have traditional sex via intercourse, he told her to: *"...find another man..."* because he no longer was one. His shame was so great, and he had shutdown so completely, he couldn't even bring himself to talk to someone who had gone through the same thing.

Since losing his erectile function, he didn't even interact with her. He'd come home from work, lay down on the couch and stare at the television, refusing to engage with her. His way of coping was total and complete disconnection.

I found this particularly sad because I knew *she* was suffering, too. They *both* needed compassion and support. Most partners of survivors know they are not the cause of their man's inability to become erect. Unfortunately, many still consider the possibility that their man's impotence is due to no longer being attracted to them. The Catch 22 here is, if the woman shows her insecurity, it can cause her partner to experience even *greater* shame. This may cause further disconnection, creating a downward spiral leading to the eventual and painful end of the relationship.

Annually, over one million men worldwide receive a diagnosis of prostate cancer and over 300,000 will lose their life to it. A large percentage of men with prostate cancer are married and cancer-induced impotence can lead to marital breakdown. Consider the scenario when a couple first receives the news that the man has prostate cancer. His partner's typical reaction is worry about how much longer he will live. Yet, for many men, the biggest concern is the possibility of losing his erectile function. These are mis-matched priorities that can lead to big problems in the bedroom.

Impotence doesn't mean loss of intimacy

Jacqueline and I discovered that impotence is not the end of sexual intimacy. In fact, it can be the start of even *greater* sexual intimacy. However, let's first examine why impotence can have such a devastating impact.

Most men equate impotence with a loss of their masculinity. The belief that a hard erection is a necessary hallmark of manhood comes from entrenched cultural influences and evolutionary wiring. If they can't perform sexually, according to procreative dictates, they must be *broken*. This is a belief that all too often causes men to feel they are no longer men, nor worthy of their mate's affection.

Losing one's ability to experience an erection is enormously difficult—a significant loss that the man and his partner must mourn. Everyone who experiences this goes through three or more of the traditional four stages of loss: *disbelief, anger, depression* and *acceptance*. Because of the importance our culture places on normal erectile function, and the lack of conversation about what else is possible (aside from pharmaceutical and surgical interventions), many men get stuck in anger and/or depression. This creates an environment in which no relationship is likely to survive. This unfortunate, ultimately unnecessary scenario, is being played out with countless couples everywhere.

The path to preserving these relationships—and experiencing greater intimacy than before—starts with *acceptance*, the last stage of the loss process. Once a man accepts the 'isness' of his impotence (i.e.

no longer fighting or resisting its reality), both he and his partner are on the threshold to healing and delightful intimate possibilities. This means no longer focusing solely on regaining erectile function. I'm not saying this endeavor is off-limits, just back off temporarily. It is *crucial* for your continued mutual sexual fulfillment to explore the many other ways of experiencing sexual intimacy beyond standard erectile-dependent, penetrative sex.

Dysfunction may mean better function

Not being able to get hard means no longer having the overwhelming urge to 'use it' that men encounter during an erection. This allows us to slow down for our partner and therefore match their sexual response profile for greater mutual satisfaction.

Thanks to my E.D., Jacqueline consistently has powerful and satisfying sexual experiences. In return, I also enjoy a much deeper level of sexual fulfillment and satisfaction. That's because I create the 'space' in which these experiences can blossom, which would otherwise be impossible if I were still fighting my condition.

The key to turning the tragedy of cancer-induced E.D. into a blessing is a *choice*. Far too many of us believe our manhood depends on external circumstances such as money, status or, more outrageously, our ability to 'perform' in bed. How damaging that belief has been.

A far more empowering choice is to define whom we are as men by how deeply we connect with and gratify our partner in ways *they* prefer. This choice is available to every man, including those affected by E.D., regardless of the cause. Relationships don't have to self-destruct because of impotence or any other physical limitation that may impact both male and female survivors. Instead, it can be the catalyst to rekindle and significantly deepen the emotional and sexual connection between couples.

Chapter 4

YOU MUST LEAP BEFORE
YOU CAN SOAR

Lion or lamb

Anyone who has cancer will tell you, each day is a balancing act between the uncertainty of where the disease may take them next, and concerns for quality of life. Sometimes, potential treatment options are available where the intended outcome is a longer life but at the expense of greatly diminished capabilities.

About a year ago, I faced such a choice, one I had been dreading for months. As those who are familiar with prostate cancer know, testosterone is its 'fuel.' For several years I took drugs that inhibited my cancer from accessing my testosterone. For a while, it worked. Then, my PSA levels rose rapidly, which meant, if we didn't do something soon, I was risking Stage 4 prostate cancer. Given half of my immediate family has succumbed to cancer of one form or another, this could mean a slow, bone-crushing, death sentence. That 'something' is chemical castration, which I thought would rob me of everything I held dear. I seriously considered accepting a much shorter life as a lion than suffering a longer one as a lamb.

I have witnessed what chemical castration has done to other men with starting T-levels far less than mine, and it's often not pretty. Besides the significant reduction of libido, other potential side effects include mood swings, hot flashes, weight gain, low energy, depression, cognitive impairment, spontaneous weeping, loss of muscle mass and lower bone density.

However, once I learned the drop in my testosterone would not be permanent, it was with the greatest trepidation that I relented and took the leap.

My testosterone roller coaster

Up to this point, my testosterone levels were off the charts, to the complete mystery of my oncologist and his referred endocrinologist. While no research exists to explain this (that I or my doctors know of anyway), I suspect it may be due to the profound intimacy Jacqueline and I enjoy. It was a virtuous cycle where the more we connect emotionally and sexually, the more my body generates testosterone, which creates additional drive for more of the same.

The following chart illustrates the history of my T-levels:

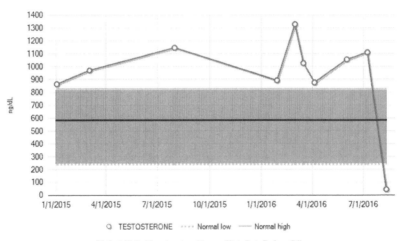

(Author's Medical Record courtesy of Sansum Clinic, Santa Barbara, CA)

These figures represent actual test results from my medical records. The shaded area represents the normal range of testosterone for healthy men of all ages. The line with circles shows my levels. The black horizontal line is where most men my age (mid-60s) reside. However, it is common for men my age to struggle with the age-related effects of *low* testosterone for which many seek hormone therapy. Also worth noting is the sudden drop of my T-levels to near zero in a matter of a few days, marking the date when I had my first injection.

I realized this treatment had the potential to significantly change my quality of life forever. For me, having those shots was akin to jumping off a cliff. I knew I had to learn how to fly or otherwise crash into the rocky crags below.

As a thought-leader, speaker and expert in advanced human sexuality and relationships, I wondered if I could continue my work with any integrity or enthusiasm. Without a sense of purpose or mission, men often slip into a pervading sense of hopelessness, an emotional state not helpful on the road to cancer recovery.

Except, it didn't quite turn out that way.

Soaring higher than ever

After almost a year of these treatments, I find my energy levels are as high as ever. Jacqueline and I still make love for hours and our emotional connection continues to deepen. Most surprisingly, despite my impotence, lack of testosterone and low libido, I have found my orgasms are now substantially stronger. A remarkable phenomenon, I believe, is available to most men going through similar treatments, something we will cover in much greater detail in later chapters.

The main side effects have been frequent hot flashes (which only help me more appreciate the resiliency of menopausal women), and reduced *urgency* in seeking my own sexual release thanks to my very low libido. Besides that, I am the same me, but with a newly humble and appreciative perspective.

Perhaps the biggest revelation during this whole process has been my unrelenting *desire* to please Jacqueline, despite my reduced need for sexual release. This means I can still give her pleasure for as long as she wants. This allows me to experience sexual fulfillment whether I climax or not.

Genuine relational and sexual fulfillment comes from unconditional giving in a space of full *Presence*, rather than seeking one's own pleasure first: an insight we share throughout this book because of its importance. This discovery is wonderful news for the millions of couples who are struggling with intimacy due to cancer, or any of life's other challenges, because circumstances cannot touch this fulfillment.

Another important lesson for me was being reminded that anticipating fear is far worse than facing it head-on. Just imagine, I almost allowed my fear to prevent me from accepting the treatments, which now extend my life.

Regardless of the relationship challenges cancer has so unkindly provided, you *can* soar above them to experience new heights of intimacy. All it requires is taking the leap of facing one's fears. This is a guaranteed way to break those invisible chains which strive mightily to keep us from living and enjoying life to its fullest.

Chapter 5

FIVE SKILLS FOR A WELL-LIVED LIFE

We only get one go-around in this adventure called life. There are no do-overs. Yet, most people struggle to live life to its fullest. I think a big part of the problem lies with the myth that our external circumstances determine whether we have a well-lived life or not. If that were true, why do so many beautiful, rich, intelligent people end up miserable?

At the tender age of 65, I've done a lot of living, doing, making terrible mistakes and hitting some levels of success. None of which ultimately mattered until I learned a well-lived life is an inside job, and has nothing to do with circumstances, abilities or luck. In looking back on my circuitous journey, I realized there were essential skills I stumbled upon, that allowed me to have a fulfilling life with Jacqueline. I share these skills with the intention that you will find something valuable for your quest.

1. **Be fully present** – for me, this skill is paramount. Being present means having the discipline to ignore everything else that vies for our attention to focus on the here and now. In our culture, where distraction is the drug of choice, Presence can be difficult to master. The best way to start is with your significant other. When with them, pretend to be an observer watching your interaction without judgment or thought. Just *observe*. With practice, you will find being the 'Observer' and being present are the same, and eventually you won't need to pretend.

2. **Be open-Hearted** – this means being willing to remove the armor we put in place to avoid emotional pain. I've learned that the Heart needs no protection (while the ego seeks it incessantly). Until we can express vulnerability in this way, we will never fully feel the pain and pleasure life offers. There is no one-way valve that blocks pain while allowing pleasure. Pain is part of this life experience. Emotional *suffering*, however, is optional, and occurs when we resist pain or unwanted circumstances which effectively turn the sufferer into a victim.

3. **Embrace uncertainty** – certainty is an illusion. As cancer survivors, we've learned this at one point or another. I'll be the first to admit I don't like uncertainty. It can cause bouts of significant anxiety. However, I have discovered when we accept and even embrace uncertainty, it can often lead to unexpected breakthroughs and positive circumstances. As long as we are alive, we will always experience uncertainty. The difference between a rich, fulfilling life and one fraught with the anxiety of what *could* happen is knowing how to manage and respond to it in a positive way.

4. **Treat everything as an adventure** – instead of seeing any circumstance as either 'good' or 'bad', consider renaming it an *adventure*. Yes, that includes dealing with cancer. You must admit the word 'adventure' is more fun and helps to create a life filled with possibilities you never imagined. It also diminishes the heaviness and charge associated with unpleasant experiences.

5. **Be clear about what you want** – intentional clarity is how I found Jacqueline. Once I opened my Heart, I could be clear about who I wanted as a life partner. With this newfound clarity, I threw myself into my *Dream Woman Project*, which took several days to complete. The result was a 13-page document describing in fine detail the woman with whom I wanted to share the rest

of my life. A year later, almost to the day, we found each other under the most unusual of circumstances, during that fateful evening in the Fall of 2012 (described earlier). She was a 100% match with what I had written. Was it Serendipity? Luck? Perhaps. Though, I suspect my total commitment to clarity and an open Heart put the odds in my favor. I've discovered the more focus and intention I put on something, the more likely it will manifest.

Is a well-lived life perfect? No. Perfection isn't attainable. However, the well-lived life is the most fulfilling one I can imagine, and certainly worth pursuing.

Chapter 6

BEING REAL

Ending shame

During my TEDx talk, I 'came out' as an impotent male who experiences extraordinary intimacy despite his condition. This is an admission men typically avoid making at all costs. I did it because it was time to end the shame. It was not just about ending my shame, but the shame of millions of other survivors and their partners who struggle in silence with this disease and the often devastating effects of treatment. Shame is one of the most useless and damaging human emotions. It occurs when others judge us and we complicity believe them.

Coming out required me to express the truth about my body and its limitations in a vulnerable way, regardless of the expectations or judgments of others. When I came out, I experienced a wonderful release of the pretenses, secrets, and lies that society prefers I maintain.

The phrase 'coming out' typically means acknowledging one's LGBTQIA orientation to the rest of the world. The term can apply to any individual or group that experiences either oppression or suppression of their identity… which means it can apply to each of us, regardless of gender or sexual orientation. What if we consider the act of coming out to mean openly acknowledging who we are regardless of what others may think? From this point on, I will use 'coming out' as a universal term that means *no longer hiding one's true self.*

Too many of us are reticent to be ourselves without inhibition because of our concern with the opinion of others. How many times have you held yourself in check out of fear, not allowing your full self-expression to emerge? This can be particularly pernicious for those dealing with the physical scarring of cancer treatments.

Coming out requires courage

To allow yourself to be and show up in the world as you are requires a heaping dose of courage. When you come out, expect resistance from others. You can also expect to experience real freedom, perhaps for the first time in your life.

When I discussed this with Jacqueline, she too had a coming out story. She came out when she told her mother that getting married and having children was not on her wish list. Thanks to her courage, she is now living the life of her dreams. She is no longer imprisoned by her culture or its expectations of women.

The bliss of not living up to other's expectations

Nature is both unbelievably wonderful and sometimes intensely cruel. Thanks to Mother Nature, we are all hard-wired for primarily one thing: *survival*. The need to survive is the relentless engine that drives evolution, diversity, and propagation. This wiring cares not one whit who or what lives or dies as long as the whole continues to grow and thrive. All species accept this existential drama without resistance or complaint—except for one… homo sapiens.

The fact that we are conscious and self-aware can disrupt the otherwise smooth-running clockwork of the survival instinct. From the moment of our birth, we depend on others for our continued existence. As we grow and develop a sense of separate identity (i.e. ego), our primal wiring causes an incessant yearning for love and approval. Without this acceptance, we innately feel the potential for abandonment by our 'tribe', which *would* mean a premature death for our distant ancestors. However, during early childhood, we don't have the emotional and intellectual capacity to distinguish between actual physical, existential threats and imagined emotional ones. So, we collapse the two. A limiting belief that carries into adulthood for most people. This explains why emotional pain can be so traumatic, since our subconscious sees it as a real threat.

Too often, because of this, we suppress our true nature by adapting to the expectations of others. Likewise, those in a position to bestow this approval and affection often make it conditional upon our conforming to *their* worldview and assigned labels.

The problem with labels is:

a) they are almost always inaccurate,

b) they can never fully capture the infinite nature of another human being, and

c) they can inflict painful emotional wounding.

You owe nothing more to the world than your authenticity. You owe nothing less to yourself than to embrace it regardless of what others may think, do or say. This resolute self-acceptance is the first step toward renewed intimacy—within the context of cancer or any of life's other challenges.

Chapter 7

THE ADVENTURE OF UNCERTAINTY

The certainty of uncertainty

I dislike uncertainty as much as anyone, perhaps more. My reaction to it can cause deep anxiety that negatively impacts my health, wealth and overall enjoyment of life: a common experience among cancer survivors and their partners. Very few things are certain in life. One is the inevitability of uncertainty. We can pretend that we have a handle on what's coming our way, but the truth is, we don't. The unexpected can happen in a heartbeat.

So why is uncertainty so universally reviled? Once again, our survival instinct seems to be the main culprit. When you don't know what's coming—or worse, when you think you know what's coming but are powerless to stop it—this can cause a deep sense of impending dread, or even doom. We are hard-wired to avoid that at all costs. The resulting anxiety is more about what we *think* can go wrong, than the actual going wrong itself. The fear of negative future outcomes is insidious; it can actually cause more harm than the object of the fear itself.

Fortunately, uncertainty has a positive side.

Turning uncertainty into possibility

Jacqueline and I have learned that if we *embrace* the 'isness' of uncertainty in our lives, it can open doors to wonderful possibilities and experiences not on our radar.

Here's are the best ways we've found to do this:

1. *Face the fear of uncertainty* – uncertainty gets the best of us when we pretend it's not there. A fear ignored is a 'death by a thousand cuts' and is far worse than one faced head-on. Fully acknowledging our fear of uncertainty is the first step.

2. *Get skilled in being present* – uncertainty is about the future and therefore it cannot touch you if you are in the present moment. While constantly living in the moment is not practical, knowing how to put yourself in that space when you experience those first pangs of anxiety can blunt their impact.

3. *See uncertainty as the threshold to possibility* – I can honestly say the best things in my life resulted from my embracing uncertainty, by jumping headfirst into the abyss of not knowing. How differently would your life unfold if you viewed uncertainty as a powerful force for positive possibilities and not just a sign of danger?

Uncertainty will always be with us, no matter what our circumstances. Fortunately, we have a choice on how to respond. Popping pills, distractions, shutting-down or playing the role of victim are some ways. Another is fully embracing uncertainty to see what adventure it may offer.

You decide which choice will best empower and prepare you and your partner to experience wondrous intimacy in this sea of uncertainty called cancer.

Chapter 8

FREEDOM FROM FEAR

The simple thought, *"I have only one year left to live..."* empowered me to live with less fear and anxiety. It showed me right away what mattered most. It's just human nature to avoid facing our mortality, but the act of doing so freed me from the clutches of self-induced fear and suffering. This has led to a more joyful, purposeful and intimate life, instead of one eclipsed by circumstances.

At some point, you too will have one year left to live. Take a moment to imagine this. What shows up and falls away may surprise you.

My greatest fear isn't death

My 65-year-old body hosts two forms of cancer: castrate-resistant prostate cancer and chronic lymphocytic leukemia (CLL). Of these two unwelcome hitchhikers, the prostate cancer, is more serious.

Having lost half of my family due to cancer, I live with the vicissitudes of my mortality every day. In my case, neither cancer marks my impending doom, but I am always on the alert for the 3rd (or 4th) shoe to drop.

Now, as you'd imagine, if a man in my predicament wakes up in the morning filled with anxiety, it concerns his health. But that isn't what used to fill me with the greatest fear. I've accepted my limited time here, and I am at peace with it. Everyone is 'terminal', it's just a matter of when and how. What has caused me the most sleep-deprivation is whether I will achieve my goals during my remaining time.

When I shifted my speaking and writing career to focus on relationships and intimacy, a whole new set of dreams and goals presented themselves. While I am aware there are no guarantees, I've been working my tail off since to realize them.

The 'Aha' that set me free

So, one morning this question bubbled up in my mind: *What if I acquired yet another form of cancer? One more aggressive and deadly—say in the liver, pancreas or brain where my doctors told me I had just 12 months left to live.* My current diagnosis and family history meant it was easy for me to consider this scenario. The interesting thing is, instead of experiencing depression or hopelessness, I felt *free.*

Here's why: when faced with a foreshortened life due to circumstances outside my control, not achieving my goals was no longer *my* fault. Whereas not achieving them, unhindered by an early demise, I viewed as a personal failure, disappointing myself and others.

Now, I see how pointless and self-punishing that whole trip had been. How I view myself as a man no longer depends upon whether I achieve my goals during my remaining time. So, I let it go. Sure, I'll continue to work toward my mission with total commitment, but without attachment to outcome. However, I suspect this new context will only help me achieve my dreams more effectively. That's because I'll be able to stay present and focused instead of dwelling in self-judgment or the fear of an unforeseeable future.

Stomping out fear

From my perspective, I see two primary types of fear: existential fear correlated with a physical threat such as cancer, and emotional fear. While existential fear helps protect our physical well-being in times of real danger, I've learned that emotional fear has no valid purpose whatsoever and is by far more insidious and debilitating.

Emotional fears feed on 'what-ifs' which, by definition, focus on the uncertainty of the future. When you focus on negative what-ifs, you have little energy left for positive and healing possibilities that can also arise out of uncertainty. However, what gives these what-ifs energy is the story our ego-driven mind creates surrounding potential negative outcomes. These stories are not real, yet when allowed to run free, they have the power to inflict emotional and even real physiological pain. To counter this, Jacqueline and I have developed an effective practice that protects us from the self-sabotage that can occur when we let these fears get the best of us.

The first thing we do is *objectify* these fears as 'cucarachas' (i.e. cockroaches in Spanish). Taking this metaphor further, we understand that these cucarachas will grow, multiply and eventually consume us if we don't stomp them the moment they show their disgusting heads.

By doing this, we no longer identify as *being* our fears, they are outside us. This allows us to be in total control of their impact on us. When either of us spots one of these cucarachas (i.e. experiences emotional fear) we will look at the floor, imagine one or more of those ugly creatures crawling around, and literally stomp our feet as we 'crush' them into oblivion. We do this without thinking. It is crucial that this reflex is automatic because thinking provides too much time for stories to form and feed the fear. As you might expect, we sometimes get strange looks when we do this in public, but we don't care. That's because concern for other people's judgments is just another cucaracha that needs squishing.

This simple reframing of how we externalize emotional fears and the exercise to stomp them into oblivion has been transformational. I cannot adequately describe the positive energy this frees up and the massive positive shift in our experience of life.

Just remember: you are *not* your fears. You have the power to crush them in an instant the moment you see them arise. This is a powerful tool to help you and your partner navigate the many relationship challenges that cancer can present on your journey to renewed intimacy.

Chapter 9

THE POWER OF GRATITUDE

Complaining sucks

No matter your station in life, you can always find reasons to complain. If you let yourself fall into that trap, life will often feel like it sucks.

We all have plenty of excuses to complain. Maybe it's our partner who just doesn't get or appreciate us, the crummy job lorded over us by an a**hole boss, inequality, inequity, politics, the weather, the news, wars, not enough money, traffic, too many people, no one notices, no one cares, life, blah, blah, blah...

Or, having cancer. Now that's a complaint most people wouldn't blame you for having. Interestingly however, I find most of the survivors I've met don't complain about their cancer.

After being a champion complainer most of my life, I realized all complaining did was make me, and those around me, *miserable*. I even complained about my own complaints. How pathetic is that? Falling into that habit, I was choosing to be a *victim* of my circumstances. Eventually, I came to realize one of the most important lessons: when life hands you something you don't like, you can either do something about it or, if that is not possible, accept it and move on. Complaining serves no one.

Antidote to complaining

The best way to break a negative habit is to replace it with a positive one.

I have found the habit of expressing gratitude for everything, even the most extreme challenges in my life, is a powerful antidote to compulsive complaining.

Gratitude expands your outlook on life; complaining contracts it. Gratitude is stress-relieving; complaining generates it. Gratitude attracts others to you; complaining drives them away. A wonderful way to bring those you love closer to you is to express gratitude about everything, even those things that appear to be challenges.

When you express genuine gratitude, you can't help but smile more. If you find your life 'sucks', chances are you are looking through the lens of complaint. Consider changing your glasses to see everything from a state of gratitude. I promise, this will amaze you as the world transforms for you, and you for it.

SECTION 2

Growing Emotional Intimacy

*"Life is not about feeling better,
it's about getting better at feeling."*

~ MICHAEL BROWN

Author of *The Presence Process*

I f you ask 10 different people what intimacy means to them, chances are you will get 10 different responses. Men tend to think about intimacy in terms of sex. In particular, intercourse. Women often equate intimacy with a deeper emotional connection. There are always exceptions of course, yet we have found significant gender-differences surrounding intimacy's meaning. These differences can become a source of conflict that could eventually result in relationship discord, stagnation or even failure.

We are very specific on how we define intimacy within this book:

Intimacy is a deep, abiding connection between two people that can occur on the emotional, sexual and spiritual levels.

The chapters within this section explore how you and your partner can grow and maintain unshakable emotional intimacy. We cover this first because no one can sustain sexual intimacy without a strong emotional connection. Emotional intimacy is the bedrock of your relationship and the foundation for enjoying and continually growing your mutual sexual intimacy and fulfillment.

Chapter 10

THE ALMOST INEVITABLE
RELATIONSHIP LIFE-CYCLE

Six stages of committed relationships

If your relationship is under siege due to loss of intimacy, the Committed Relationship Life-cycle model[7] can help you identify how and why you have come to this unfortunate place.

Most committed relationships travel through a predictable arc where, over-time, each partner's sense of fulfillment changes. If a couple stays together until they reach retirement age, two common outcomes are possible: a rekindling of intimacy or relationship failure (reflected in physical separation or just settling).

Unfortunately, the failure mode is by far the most likely outcome for most couples. These consequences are more likely when external stressors, such as cancer, challenge the relationship.

There are innate forces that powerfully impact every aspect of intimate relationships—forces that, if left unchecked, almost guarantee partners will lose the mutual fulfillment that initially brought them together. Thankfully, a way to avoid this unhappy outcome is available.

The first step to stem loss of fulfillment is becoming aware of where you are in the relationship life-cycle and identifying the negative influences that have hampered your relationship. When you can take the

---

7 This model was developed exclusively by the authors for the purpose of identifying and explaining the six stages most committed relationships go through over their lifetime and is based upon their observations.

appropriate steps to correct these influences and change the associated behaviors, you'll see an immediate increase in fulfillment within your relationship.

The following chart depicts the six primary stages that impact committed partners' experience of mutual fulfillment.

Committed Relationship Life-cycle
Default Sexual Operating System

Here's a more detailed explanation of each stage:

1. **Courtship** – the 'getting-to-know-each-other' stage. Often experienced as an exciting adventure accompanied with the potential promise of a wonderful and fulfilling life together. My courtship with Jacqueline didn't start until we established a deep level of emotional intimacy and friendship. Thinking back, it began the night we first went out dancing. That is when I kissed her the first time after returning her home.

2. **Honeymoon** – assuming courtship leads to commitment, couples enter the well-known honeymoon stage. For the majority of couples, this represents the pinnacle of their mutual emotional and sexual fulfillment, lasting anywhere from a few weeks to several years. Shortly after our first romantic weekend, I was on my way to Brazil. However, when I came back two weeks

later to be with Jacqueline for Christmas, that was very much our honeymoon period. I think we spent about 80% of our time making love for countless hours, never getting tired and always reaching new heights. Yet, for reasons revealed in later chapters, this still represents the low point of our relationship's sexual fulfillment, which has continued to get better the longer we are together.

3. **Internal stressors** – once the thrill of the honeymoon period wears off, routine, distraction and gender differences can erode mutual fulfillment. We call these 'internal stressors' because each partner has control over them. What's interesting is that Jacqueline and I rarely experience these kinds of stressors because we are aware and know how to overcome them when and if they arise. We will share more on this later in the book.

4. **External stressors** – significant further diminishment of mutual satisfaction can occur due to external stressors such as career, finances, health issues, and in particular, having children. Without appropriate checks and balances in place, these have the potential of creating deep emotional wounding between partners. This creates a subsequent and proportional impact to their sense of emotional and sexual fulfillment. Jacqueline and I have our share of these—especially within the context of my two cancers and the rigors of our respective careers. With that said, by using the tools we cover in this book, our relationship easily mitigates these and only continues to grow stronger.

It is common to seek high levels of personal fulfillment surrounding one's children or career, while your relationship wanes. In fact, a *big* trap is to use external fulfillment as a distraction or replacement for the lack of intimacy in one's relationship. This happened in my previous marriage. Once the emotional wounding became so pronounced, we could no longer find fulfillment within the relationship. My ex-wife focused most of her energy nurturing our children, while I worked harder than ever to support the family. Society sanctions and admires both pursuits, so I told myself. Besides putting the last nail into the coffin of our marriage, we also modeled for our children how *not* to express healthy emotional intimacy within a committed relationship.

5. **Stagnation** – where partners are just holding things together, hopefully long enough for the external stressors to pass (i.e. retirement, kids leave home, etc.). Couple's often seek therapy to address long-brewing conflicts as well as the lack of intimacy and sexual fulfillment during this stage. Unfortunately, like so many other baby-boomer couples, my marriage's stagnation eventually led to divorce. At that point, no amount of therapy could have helped (a sentiment we've heard from therapists as well). As one very experienced marriage counselor put it, by the time they see couples at this stage, they know the chances for reconciliation are slim.

6. **Maturation** – in most cases, the final stage of the relationship cycle, and it has three possible outcomes:

   a) **Rekindling** – when the partners re-ignite the love and passion they had during the earlier stages of their union. However, this rarely leads to achieving the same levels of fulfillment experienced during the honeymoon stage.

   b) **Settling** – one version of relationship failure where couples stay together out of convenience. Some couples choose this route either for financial reasons or unwillingness to get out of their comfort zone and start over again, which is what would happen if they left their current relationship.

c) **Termination** – the ultimate form of relationship breakdown where a couple ends the relationship due to unresolvable conflict and deep emotional wounding.

It is important to note that the maturation stage can occur any time after the honeymoon stage. Also, both internal and external stressors are cumulative and ongoing. For example, just because a couple transitions from internal stressors to external, the internal stressors don't just go away. In fact, unless pro-actively addressed, they only become more toxic.

This makes one wonder why most committed relationships follow this progression and what they can do to avoid this fate.

The default human Sexual Operating System

The human Sexual Operating System[8] (S.O.S.) is a collection of genetic and culturally based *drives*, *beliefs* and *behaviors*, primarily for the purpose and support of procreation; it has a significant influence on nearly all aspects of intimate relationships. It is an advanced model of human intimate behavior that successfully predicts the stages and potential outcomes of typical committed relationships. Its significant power to impact relationship behavior and outcomes is due to our inherent procreative imperative—collective survival of the species, irrespective of any desire for children.

Jacqueline and I sum up the S.O.S.'s impact on intimate relationships this way:

The way men and women are biologically and culturally 'wired', gets in the way of the deeper emotional, sexual and spiritual intimacy for which their Hearts yearn.

The largely unconscious influence of the default S.O.S. waylays most couple's efforts to achieve deep connection and intimacy. With

---

8 The Sexual Operating System is an internally-consistent, advanced model of human intimate behavior developed by the authors.

that said, the value of a good model doesn't start and end with its predictive powers. It should also provide insight on how to achieve *positive* outcomes. This means having a committed relationship in which mutual fulfillment continues to *improve* over time, rather than diminish.

The Sexual Operating System model provides us with this ability. Imagine your honeymoon as the *starting point* of your mutual fulfillment. As incredible as our honeymoon was, it represents the *low point* of our ongoing mutual fulfillment as a committed couple. As difficult as it may be to accept, Jacqueline and I are living proof. The following chart illustrates our continuing experience:

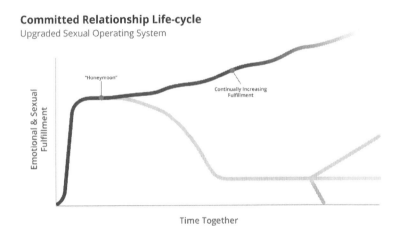

Granted, we have our ups and downs too. For example, when we moved to our new residence, I started my oral chemo the day after finishing that stressful relocation. This treatment protocol had a significant impact on my immune system, and I caught the granddaddy of all flu bugs. My condition worsened to the point I had to go to the local hospital emergency room twice in two days resulting in admission on the 2nd day. Jacqueline was beside herself, wondering if I would even survive.

This experience brought up every primal fear each of us had and put a huge strain on our relationship. Yet, because we could step outside these difficult circumstances using our chosen context of Heart vs. ego (where our egos were experiencing all the fear and doubt), we could work through them in a way that strengthened our relationship. This is an important shift in context that will be covered before the end of this section.

We both consciously apply our knowledge of the default S.O.S. to the point we have been able to 'upgrade' it. By upgrading our S.O.S. we have learned to leverage these inherent drives and change our beliefs and behaviors, resulting in a virtuous upward spiral of increasing fulfillment. This doesn't imply that we are immune to internal and external stressors, it means our understanding of these inherent forces empowers us to mitigate issues before they cause lasting damage.

Your relationship firewall

By learning about your S.O.S. and how to upgrade it, you can create a nearly impenetrable firewall, protecting your relationship from ultimate failure. We have found that the S.O.S. is also profoundly useful in mitigating cancer's impact on intimacy. We will cover the specifics of how you can upgrade your respective Sexual Operating Systems at the end of Section 3.

The S.O.S. model of human intimate behavior is a powerful and fundamental breakthrough for committed relationships. This knowledge is best used to *prevent* emotional wounding from causing irreparable damage to your relationship. Think of emotional wounding as little cracks that form within the ego. The ego has great difficulty handling anything it perceives to be a threat, whether physical or emotional. So once the wounding occurs, the ego puts up protective armor to prevent further pain. The more armor that forms, the more your emotional intimacy suffers. When this happens, it often signals the beginning of the end of the relationship.

An upgraded S.O.S. helps both partners avoid or heal these little wounds before they turn into gaping ones. It also provides a path to ever-increasing levels of mutual fulfillment. However, the S.O.S. is *not* well-suited to fix relationships that have suffered severe damage caused by deep divides.

Clearly, the shift in beliefs and behaviors necessary to sustain and grow your relationship fulfillment is far less costly than suffering the almost inevitable outcome of a typical relationship life-cycle.

Chapter 11

LIVING HEART-OPEN

How does one go from being shutdown most of their adult life to living Heart-open and deeply connected? For me, it requires doing one simple daily exercise to keep me in my Heart. As a side benefit, it also opens the Hearts of others—in 10 seconds or less. Given its simplicity, it may tempt one to think it couldn't be that easy. Trust me on this one, if it works for me (a real hard case), it will for you too.

"Can't you be human just once in your life!"
That was the refrain shouted by my wife as she entered advanced labor with our second child at the hospital. Instead of paying attention and comforting her, I was arguing with our four-year-old daughter about something unimportant. Her rebuke wasn't just labor pain rage. It reflected my typical lack of empathy—not uncommon for shutdown or disconnected individuals.

Her anger stung deep because there was more than an element of truth to it. Despite success in business and being a high-energy extrovert, something always seemed amiss in my life. I couldn't seem to connect genuinely with anyone, including my wife and kids.

Don't get me wrong, I could converse with the best of them and make people laugh—but I did it devoid of any semblance of vulnerability. Despite years of therapy, I was no closer to the answer, which just made me more frustrated and disconnected.

Heart-opening transformation

One day I declared: *"Enough is enough..."* and pulled the trigger on changing my life forever. With the help of someone who saw the real me (despite all attempts to hide), the source of my disconnect became abundantly clear; a fierce unwillingness to show my Heart, express vulnerability and feel everything. Thanks to childhood wounds, I had placed a ton of armor around my Heart to protect it from ever being hurt again. All it did was prevent me from feeling *anything* or connecting with *anyone.*

This realization was one of the biggest moments of my life. From that point on, I vowed to stay vulnerable and Heart-open. I cannot overstate the impact of that choice. Because of this spiritual and emotional shift, I experienced *immediate* changes. My face softened, my eyes sparkled with joy, and I experienced being truly alive for the first time. People who had known me for decades commented that I looked 20 years younger. Imagine Scrooge's transformation after his visit with the Spirit of Christmas Future. That was me. This probably explains why I always burst out sobbing at that point in the book when I read it to my kids every Christmas. My Heart *ached* for that possibility, which only required me to have the courage to allow it to happen. I assure you, *all* of our Hearts want the same.

That Heart transformation happened two months *before* my diagnosis. I sincerely believe I'd be dead now if I hadn't taken that step. Opening my Heart saved my life and helps me daily to overcome the many challenges of my two ongoing cancers.

Open your Heart by giving one away

However, the waves of life continue to test me, making it easy to hide my Heart again. To ensure I never backslide, I carry little glass hearts everywhere. They are nothing special, just inexpensive iridized glass from China. However, what I do with them is what keeps my Heart open. Almost daily, I give them to random people I meet. I never know with whom I will share them or why I let my intuition and Heart be my guide.

I give these little glass hearts to men, women, and children of all ages. As I look into their eyes, I give them a heart and say: *"This is for you because you have such a big, beautiful Heart."* Yes, I do this for men too. This simple act deeply touches most of the people who receive them. You might think some people may not be open to receiving this unique acknowledgment from a stranger. In all the years I've practiced this, only two declined to accept. One was an older lady with a walker who was about to cross a busy intersection. I got the impression she had concerns about falling if she took her hands off that walker to receive my offering.

The other instance was far more poignant. I was in the cancer center infusion room waiting to receive a shot that would leave me chemically castrated as part of my prostate cancer treatment. After asking permission of the attending nurses if it would be okay to visit the other infusion patients, my eye caught one in particular. She was an older, stately looking woman. As I approached, her face gave evidence she was struggling with something other than the procedure. When I introduced myself and offered to give her the heart, she responded with: *"No, give it to someone who has a heart!"* This confirmed my suspicion she was dealing with something beyond cancer.

As we spoke more, she shared her colorful and impressive life in public service. When it was time for me to go, I said: *"Here, maybe you can give it to someone else who is deserving."* With that she accepted my gift. On my next visit to the infusion room, I asked the nurse about that woman and how she was doing. She remembered her and that incident well. She said after I left that patient was uncharacteristically chatty and smiling. Before leaving she gave that nurse the heart. Although she only had it for a few hours, it caused a significant shift in her spirit.

Another time, I gave one to a fellow who I approached in a parking lot because he had a Ducati motorcycle which I was admiring. After discussing his bike for a while I had this urge to give him a heart. He had a quiet presence that moved me to connect with him this way. That simple act of giving seemed to touch him.

I ran into him again at a coffee shop the next day. He said: *"Do you remember me?"* At first, I didn't but then a smile of recognition came across my face as I said: *"You're the Ducati guy!"* He replied: *"That's right. You know that heart you gave me yesterday? Well, I went to the beach afterward for a walk and met someone and gave it to her. I think there may be something there."* Apparently so, because Ducati guy (with whom I have since become friends), and his new girlfriend are still together after three years.

This simple act of connecting Hearts by giving them away has served me as much as it serves the people to whom I give them. Perhaps, even more. I've discovered I cannot give these hearts without my Heart being wide open. Ten seconds is all it takes, yet the impact can last a lifetime. I have not found a simpler way for me to stay Heart-open even in the most trying of circumstances. With this exercise, I have been able to overcome challenges that used to cause me to disconnect and put barriers up again.

Whether you use glass hearts or other acts of selfless giving, you will find this to be a powerful and consistent way to keep your Heart open to giving and receiving love unconditionally. Heart-open is a state of being, fundamental to maintaining genuine emotional intimacy and connection with anyone, especially your significant other. This powerful bit of wisdom took me 60 years to realize, but it changed everything about the fulfillment of my life as a whole. However old you are, it's never too late to incorporate this into your life. It will instantly change your experience of life into one of celebrating genuine connection with others.

Chapter 12

NO SUCH THING AS
A BROKEN HEART

A context that changes everything

Jacqueline and I view the Heart as our true, unadulterated non-physical/ spiritual essence. Some philosophies refer to this as the *Soul*, *Higher Self* or *Consciousness*. For our purposes here, we simply refer to it as our Heart.

Despite conventional wisdom, the Heart is always at peace, never changes, can never hurt or break and is never needy or jealous. Heart is where true, lasting connection with others originates. In fact, any negative qualities attributed to the Heart are actually from the realm of ego. So, next time someone says: *"She/He broke my Heart!"*, consider re-framing it as: *"She/He broke my ego!"* When you re-frame negative aspects of your relationships this way, it greatly diminishes any charge around it.

In the simplest terms, we believe human beings have a dual experience of reality: the head-based reality (a mental construct, i.e. ego, the voice in our head), and the Heart (our core essence, which goes beyond the physical or intellectual). The Heart, the Observer, *is* our Awareness. Ego, or the false self, comes into existence in early childhood and its primary purpose is survival. Experiences during this vulnerable period shape the ego, which expresses itself through personality.

Keep in mind, this duality is just a context through which we view reality. We are not saying it's true, just that Jacqueline and my relationship thrives because of it. Consider temporarily suspending any preconceptions or judgments and continue reading. This may well be the most important insight you receive from this book.

Egos in love

When we fall in love with someone, entertain the possibility that our ego is doing the falling. I am not denying that a deeper, ineffable connection is also there. However, the flirting, charm and much of the infatuation come from the ego.

"OMG, I'm so in love with him/her!!!"

Does that sound familiar? Our ego can get excited when connecting with someone who fulfills most of our relationship needs. If the feelings are not mutual, it trashes the ego. In fact, you could say our egos manifest the stereotypical definition of love, which, if left unchecked, becomes the source of relationship conflict. These fractured dynamics occur with couples everywhere and at all ages.

A young female friend asked me for relationship advice. She was reluctant to tell her boyfriend how much she cared for him.

I asked her: *"What are you afraid will happen if you tell him how you feel?"*

"That he won't feel the same about me."

"What would happen if he didn't?" I asked.

"It would devastate me!" she said with a hint of fear in her voice.

Who hasn't been in this precarious position, afraid to share the depth of our feelings with someone special, in fear of rejection and not wanting to have our 'hearts broken'?

'Brokenhearted' is the common vernacular that sums up the drama and deep loss that describes the end of a relationship. For many people, the fear of a 'broken heart' prevents them from beginning a new relationship that might bring the greatest joy they've ever known.

Although it's painful to have one's ego hurt, that experience does not inherently do permanent damage. If we can see conflict, or even the end of a relationship as a matter of a wounded ego, that helps lessen our fear of authenticity. This shift in context becomes a relationship 'safety net', making it easier to risk authenticity, vulnerability and open-Heartedness.

I wanted my friend to get it, so I continued to probe: *"If your boyfriend didn't return your feelings, what would hurt—your ego... or your Heart?"*

She didn't quite know how to respond.

"What if the true essence of who you are, your Heart, could never experience hurt? What if your ego experiences all the pain and suffering? Within this context, the worst that could happen is that your boyfriend may trash your ego, but he cannot in any way, harm your Heart."

She considered this for a few moments and then asked: *"You mean if my ego gets hurt, I should just shut down my Heart?"* Not a surprising question, considering our culture's habit of shutting down to avoid intense emotions.

"Quite the opposite," I answered. *"Should he not reciprocate your feelings, try observing the wounding of your ego from the perspective of your open Heart. Think of it as standing back and watching your ego being mangled in a slow-motion car crash. From this perspective, the damage done will only seem like an out-of-body experience when you realize that your ego is not the real you."*

"The essence of who you are, your Heart, is not part of the crash, so it isn't hurt. Your Heart is still alive and available. The Heart merely observes the drama as it unfolds. Does this change anything for you?"

"I guess I'm not so afraid anymore" she said.

The next day, my friend reported back that this one simple distinction transformed how she saw her relationship. It freed her up to be authentic with her boyfriend. She became a big believer in our intimacy coaching work because of the immediate impact this simple shift in context provided her.

Our biggest test

We know it works. It helps Jacqueline and I daily. About one year into our relationship, Jacqueline was having doubts that I was the man for her. This was primarily due to my choice to leave a lucrative career as an international technology speaker for one of great uncertainty devoted to helping others with issues surrounding sex, intimacy and relationships. The possibility of Jacqueline not sharing my life was too painful to consider. Yet, for a few days, I thought our relationship was ending. Though she often said she loved me, I could sense an impenetrable wall separating us. I craved a much deeper connection than she appeared willing to give.

I adored this woman, and my relationship with her had been instrumental in my continued spiritual and emotional transformation. My ego was beside itself with fear. My state of shock registered prominently in the white pallor of my face. I was dealing with old issues of abandonment, loss, and hopelessness. Yet, despite my greatest fears, I knew I had to let her go if she was not willing to show up vulnerable and open-Hearted with me.

So, one evening I asked her over for a face-to-face no BS meeting. As I sat across from her, I became quiet and connected with my Heart—the Heart that would continue to love her without reservation even if she chose to leave. Before I spoke, my Heart dispassionately watched as my ego was ripped, limb from limb, while staring into the abyss of a life without her.

"Sweetie," I said finally, *"I love you without reservation. You are the one with whom I want to spend the rest of my life. I know you care for me too. I sense however, you have an invisible wall between us and that does not work for me. You are all in or not. I'm not willing to accept part way. If you can't give total commitment to our relationship, I will respect that and love you no matter where life takes you. The choice is yours."*

When I finished, she was quiet with a solemn look on her face. She took several days to return with an answer. During this period my ego was in utter agony yet my Heart was serene. This episode was our biggest test yet for this empowering shift of perspective.

As you may have suspected by now, Jacqueline was going through her ego vs. Heart struggle as well...

Let me demonstrate how deeply social programming runs and how it can shape how we behave.

As I shared earlier, the most influential person in my life is my mother. In her defense, she never actually said: *"When you find 'the one', make sure he is financially secure and has a certain level of qualifications."* However, she would make remarks about others that clearly sunk into my consciousness. She would say things like: *"So-and-so married so-and-so... she's sharp to make that decision!"* Or: *"So-and-so married her boyfriend, who is a total loser. Look at his low paying job! What a shame."*

I grew up with those recordings playing in my head. Every time I found someone I liked, inadvertently I'd compare them to the 'ideal' mate of which my mother spoke. If the guy didn't match up, I felt short-changed.

Authentically exploring the self is paramount to weather the disappointments that drive our actions and reactions in any relationship. From our socio-cultural imprint and past relationship experiences, we acquire systems of belief which direct our behavior outside our awareness. It is not possible to build a healthy relationship without first bringing these limiting beliefs to light.

These beliefs caused their greatest damage when I picked someone who was not 'ideal.' That comes with the heavy emotional burden of having made a mistake. This weight would show in my behavior, and then the guy would notice and eventually we would both be miserable. I would then justify my struggle with the thought that I could turn him into my mother's image of the ideal mate. Everyone knows, you can't change anyone; you accept them the way they are or your relationship will not be a happy one.

It was early in our relationship when Michael and I almost broke up. When I saw Michael on weekends, the tape of my mom's voice would play something like this: *"This guy doesn't even own a house. It's pathetic you are falling for him when he doesn't own the roof over his head."* Of course, it didn't matter I didn't own a house, either! I really thought it was okay if the woman didn't own a house, because the man should be the one to provide it. This was the twisted set of beliefs I held dear until Michael confronted me by saying: *"Jacqueline, you aren't here."* Meaning, I wasn't fully present and committed to our relationship. He also sensed an inconsistency in how I was showing up, as in: *"You say, you love me, yet you are distant."*

I so admired his courage to insist our relationship must be all in or not at all. That was the moment I faced my fears and questioned the belief system by which I had lived my whole life. With this affront, I practiced new behaviors congruent with the real me who was emerging. It was me being reborn. It continues to amaze me how I had been numb to my true longing to give and receive love and contribute to the world. I now have that life. By shifting me away from my ego-driven existence, Michael gently awakened me to a place of unconditional love and compassion.

Clearly, for this to happen in any relationship, each partner needs to be on the same path of living authentically.

Ego, the eclipse of the Heart

Relationship troubles start when we allow our ego to eclipse our Heart, blocking its ability to give and receive true connection with our significant other. That is clearly what happened with Jacqueline and I in that situation. The Heart is like the sun, always shining, always pouring out endless warmth and connection. We call it Love with a capital 'L' when this profound and transcendent connection occurs. Ego forges the armor we use to protect ourselves from emotional wounding. It deceives us into believing this armor is there to shield our Heart when it's only trying to protect itself. In so doing, it only serves to block the Heart from fulfilling its highest purpose.

When someone we love hurts us, we tend to shut down or withdraw. That is our hurt ego putting its armor around our Heart to create a greater sense of self and separation. Just know, your Heart continues to shine unabated. Once you accept that, you have a head start in managing the unlimited expression of your Heart with the inconsolable needs of the ego.

Awareness, the great mediator

What would happen if you took the time to notice your ego's machinations by standing back and seeing how the need to survive and create separation with your partner drives the ego? Once you develop the discipline to observe dispassionately your relationship from the context of ego, you're in a position to interrupt the ego's reactive tendencies. By doing that, you eliminate drama from your relationship. When conflicts arise, they will be short-lived.

Does this mean becoming aware and adapting this Heart-centric context will ensure your relationship will survive? Not necessarily. There may come a point when the best interest of both parties is to move on due to separate paths of individual growth. However, if it comes to that, through your awareness, you will release each other out of Love, rather than ego-based need and conflict. Ego sees this mutual emancipation as a form of death, while Heart celebrates what was, is, and is yet to come. The ego never stops, but that doesn't mean it has to be in the driver's seat. By being aware, the Heart becomes your navigator. When your Heart is your guide, you will never go astray.

From that near relationship-ending experience, Jacqueline

and I witnessed, once again, that the Heart gives and receives love unconditionally. It is never needy, jealous or insecure, nor can anyone hurt or break it. The ego is always seeking reciprocity to fuel its sense of separate identity. The ego reacts to anything that threatens its existence or sense of importance. As relationships come and go, the Heart remains constant and unwavering while the ego is an endless roller coaster ride providing thrill and terror.

Is it true our Heart is our essence and only ego can feel emotional pain? This is just one perspective. This context is no more or less true than the popular notion of broken-Heartedness. You are free to choose which one works best for you.

Ask yourself, which context empowers you to love fully without reservation? Which context frees you to explore new relationships fearlessly? Which one enslaves you to numbness and the less-than-lofty goal of avoiding pain?

All human beings have the power to choose, just as my friend whom I coached did. Just know, if you opt for this more empowering context, your ego will put up a huge fight—a fight from which, we sincerely hope your Heart will emerge victorious. If it does, your relationship will transform permanently for the better.

Chapter 13

DELICIOUS DISCOVERY

Don't kill the thrill

Think about your relationship. How long was it before you knew your partner completely? Likely not long at all. Now, consider the possibility your comprehensive bundle of 'knowing' is only the *tip* of the iceberg. Imagine 90% of who they are remains undiscovered. A simple way exists to keep each other in the throes of delicious discovery, whether you've been together for 5 months or 50 years. A way that leads to an ongoing adventure that seems like you just met, every single day of your lives.

Humans have a proclivity for labeling everything, including other people. The reason for this tendency is straightforward. The act of labeling provides us with a perceived sense of certainty in an uncertain world. Whenever you meet someone for the first time, chances are your label-making machine (your ego), goes into overdrive. You subconsciously name and categorize every aspect of that person. You assess their physical appearance, personality, habits, values and so on. The more effort you put in, the more refined and nuanced these labels become. This continues until at some point an internal switch flips, signifying you sufficiently know this other being and no longer need to be open to discovering anything new about them.

That is the moment you have cut yourself off from the rest of their possibilities. It is also the moment you are at risk of taking the other for granted. Categorizing people this way is certainly convenient because it's efficient, requires the least amount of effort and frees you up for other things. The downside is it's boring as hell. Another word for this boredom is *autopilot*. Relationships that slip into autopilot mode can eventually go off the rails.

This insight came to Jacqueline and I quite by surprise. We'd both been in previous relationships that dissolved into stultifying routine and severe lack of fulfillment. This go-around, we have resolved to avoid this slow relationship death at all costs. We now find our relationship provides a powerful space for each of us to manifest and express aspects of ourselves we weren't even previously aware of. Much to our delight, we continue to discover new things about each other and ourselves.

If any two people in a committed relationship can say they know each other it would be us—thanks to our unrelenting commitment to authenticity. Yet, almost without fail, during tender moments, I look into Jacqueline's eyes, and have this strange, yet wonderful, feeling that I barely know her. I know that, in truth, I'm only seeing a glimpse of the vast expanse of who she is. When it first happened, I found this feeling unsettling. That's because my ego doesn't like surprises. Interestingly, when I first mentioned this to her, she said she had the same experience with me. I pondered about this because it's unlike anything she or I had ever encountered. Then, it occurred to us that the key to this incredible and continuing phenomenon was the fact that we were both *present* for each other.

Adventure in the state of Presence

Presence is the state of deep awareness free from labeling, judgment, expectations or needs. Presence is a place where a fundamental part of who we are lives beyond the ego, where we simply bear witness to one another. This creates a space for both of us to express fully who we are, including aspects of ourselves we didn't previously suspect exist. It is within this space the beautiful adventure of our relationship continues to unfold.

Many couples strive for familiarity because it provides certainty. At first glance, inviting unexpected aspects of your partner into the relationship can seem threatening. *What if a new facet you don't like emerges? What if it signals it may be time to go separate ways?* In most cases, it won't, but with an open Heart, it could expose a whole new area for both to explore. That's why we call life an adventure. Anything else is just a guided tour.

Imagine for a moment how freeing it would be to embrace what unfolds rather than fearing it. When you accept you are not your ego, you will discover something much greater—something everlasting— always unfolding within each of you. This is a profoundly empowering context in which to navigate the dynamics of your relationship. By accepting the expanse of these possibilities, you have access to aspects of each other that are not even on your respective radars. If you keep an adventurous spirit within a state of mutual Presence, your relationship will forever be on a journey of wondrous discovery.

Chapter 14

EIGHT HABITS FOR HIGHLY SUCCESSFUL RELATIONSHIPS

As we previously said, Jacqueline and I are well beyond the honeymoon period. Yet our sexual intimacy, relationship fulfillment, and emotional connection continue to hit new heights. From this perspective, we'd like to share eight habits we practice to achieve this ever-increasing fulfillment we enjoy:

1. *Give daily gratitude* – we have found gratitude to be an effective antidote to negativity. The first thing we do upon waking is give sincere, heartfelt gratitude for each other being in our lives. We also give gratitude for life's many blessings and challenges. We express gratitude for our challenges because they help us become stronger.

2. *Meditate* – this is another 'first' each morning. Our world is very frenetic and has many distractions vying for our attention. We each spend a few minutes in the morning quieting our monkey-minds and re-centering. This helps prepare us for the next very important habit…

3. *Be present* – this one is crucial. Jacqueline and I insist on being present for one another whenever we are together. Whether we are eating a meal, listening to music, having fun, walking on the beach, kissing, saying goodbye or making love, we stay

fully aware of each other. We have found Presence is the only way our relationship can continue to flourish. Although we are busy professionals, we always make time to create a space of Presence. Without this practice, we know we will pay the hefty price of disconnection.

4. **Be authentic** – we insist on always showing up as our authentic selves and saying what is on our minds without pretense or fear of the other's feelings being hurt. This gives us confidence that the other is not hiding or holding anything back. This is a fearless, deep knowing that includes everything from the full range of ugly warts to the indescribable beauty that reveals the endless wonder of the other.

   Jacqueline is particularly good about this. Since English is her fourth language, she can sometimes come off as too direct, without understanding the nuances native speakers often use to buffer the impact of their words. I find this refreshing because I know where she stands, and that she is not holding back on anything that may turn into a bigger charge that erupts later. Imagine how freeing it would be for each of you to communicate *authentically*. There would be no more energy spent trying to figure out what your partner is really saying.

5. **Separate the ego from the Heart** – as mentioned many times throughout this book, we love each other under the context our Heart, not our ego, is our true essence. This allows us to take any relationship pain and not make it personal. Any pain we experience simply reflects our ego. This habit makes conflicts rare, and, when they happen, relatively easy to mend. Just like any other couple, we have our share of struggles. The difference is we are cognizant of how our egos create and sustain any charge that occurs, and through this awareness apply this context. This process makes it much easier for us to defuse the

charge and resolve the conflict. It is a process that strengthens our relationship every time it happens.

6. **Respect gender differences** – we acutely know our hard-wired, gender-based emotional and sexual differences. With this knowledge, we strive to adjust our respective behaviors so these differences no longer rob the intimacy and fulfillment we have built. For example, I understand that when Jacqueline shares a problem, she isn't looking for me to fix it. Instead, she wants me to be present and hear her. Likewise, she understands that because I am a man, I like to feel appreciated for the things I do. Sexually, for her to reach her full sensual potential during lovemaking, I need to slow down and let her arousal build in the time she requires. Couples ignorant of these differences—or worse, couples who ignore them—invite serious trouble.

7. **Maintain separate lives** – this is perhaps the most controversial of the eight habits. While we live in the same home, we each have our own bedroom. Friday through Sunday nights we sleep together, while the rest of the week, we sleep in our own beds. We believe part of the success of our relationship is because we maintain our individuality. To continue growing as individuals, we each need space, figuratively and literally. Our respective time apart to grow doesn't scare us. This also means, when together, we are much more excited and present for each other.

Another related consideration is that we respect each other's privacy and belongings. I don't go into Jacqueline's room without permission and vice versa. One time, I inadvertently discovered an item of hers she hid in her pillowcase on her side of my bed. When I mentioned this to her, she accused me of violating her private space. Here's why...

When Michael and I were about to move in together, I brought a few hundred dollars in cash over to his place. In the rush of preparing for the move, I put the money on my side of the bed, underneath my pillow. I forgot all about it. In my mind, I had put my money in a place I considered 'my turf.' I expected to find this cash exactly where I put it. End of story.

The next day, as Michael made the bed, he found the stack of my money. Loudly, he said: *"What's this money doing here, is this yours?"*

First of all, I felt like such an idiot for leaving money where it didn't belong. The fact that I forgot about it, made me look like a careless person. I immediately played the self-judgment tape: *"What if he thinks I'm an irresponsible person? Blah, blah."*

Secondly, I justified it to myself by thinking that the pillow was my territory. At that point, I was angry with him, and myself for allowing this embarrassing situation to happen, just as we were preparing to move in together. Michael upset me because I felt he violated 'my area', something I fiercely protect. It didn't matter that this was *his* home, and he had every right to make the bed. Still because of this minor drama I questioned our decision to live together. The voice in my head was saying, *"This is not looking good."*

After the blow-up, we talked through the whole scene with cool heads. We both needed to understand why we acted and reacted the way we did. After much conversation and sharing our authentic truths, we decided not to let this silly incident upset our future. This entire episode was comprised of nothing more than stories in our head, stoked by fear. One more cucaracha to stomp on so we could move forward with living together.

The way we defused this minor riff, which could have grown

into a major one, was to first acknowledge the charge each of our egos felt. Then we discussed it within the context and space of being Heart-open. For handling other, less pressing, issues, we developed an innovative relationship tool: our last habit.

8. **Hold MasterHeart meetings** – periodically, during the quiet of Sunday evenings, Jacqueline and I hold what we call MasterHeart meetings. 'MasterHeart' is a take on the Master Mind meetings described in the book *Think & Grow Rich* by Napoleon Hill. The primary purpose of these meetings is to discuss anything that may become a source of conflict or wounding. This can only happen when each partner communicates in a non-threatening and loving manner. It is important that any words spoken never land as criticism, only a genuine way to help each other become better partners. We also recommend each partner take a moment to express sincere gratitude for the other.

After doing this for several months, we realized that most couples may benefit from this structured coming together. That's because it encourages each person to dedicate time to be present for the most important person in their life. We use a template to guide us during these meetings to help keep us focused and avoid going off on tangents. You can download a free copy of this template via our CancerIntimacyHelp.com website.

Will incorporating these habits fix a broken relationship? Not likely, nor are they designed for that purpose. Ideally, you practice them *before* your relationship is beyond repair. Will doing these faithfully guarantee your relationship will flourish and never fail? Not necessarily. However, we believe they will significantly decrease your chances of relationship failure and establish a firm foundation upon which your sense of mutual fulfillment will continue to grow.

Chapter 15

PRETENSE HURTS

Into-me-see

Emotional intimacy is foundational to any successful long-term relationship and requires giving permission to allow others to see the real you. Pretense prevents this from happening. People use pretense out of fear for how people may judge them if they showed their authentic self. If you can relate to this, ask yourself what part of you is fearing being authentic? Your ego or your Heart?

This suggests a straightforward, but not necessarily easy way to avoid pretense forever. Having a relationship based on authenticity required me to recognize the distinction between my ego and my Heart. Once again, we are not saying this duality is true, just that it continues to be a very empowering context through which Jacqueline and I view life. Thanks to this context, we experience our fears as existential threats to our egos, rather than our timeless selves. This significantly reduces the fear of being authentic with anyone.

Now, does this mean we don't experience the pain or sting of wounding? Of course not. However, we prefer to be aware and feel everything rather than pretend that the pain or fear is not there. This approach also helps with the concern of hurting someone we love by telling them the truth. That fear stems more from how we think they will react—that they'll become angry or abandon us. If you want your relationship to always grow and blossom, avoid pretense. Once you cross the threshold of authenticity, your significant relationships and your life will become easier and incredibly more fulfilling.

From the first moment you meet

Relationship pretense often starts the moment two people first meet. It's almost a cliché how individuals show only the best side of their physical, emotional and intellectual attractiveness. Most of us have a refined and intuitive truth detector that can sense pretense, yet many remain unaware of its warnings or just ignore them. That's because the strident needs of the ego easily drown out its quiet voice.

Many couples pretend that everything is okay in their relationship when it's anything but that. There are always rational reasons for maintaining pretenses. These rationalizations often include: protecting the kids, not hurting each other's feelings or avoiding the financial and emotional strain that can come with a breakup.

Relationship pretense fools no one: not your close friends, your kids, or even, deep down, yourself. Pretense is not a useful coping mechanism, and neither is staying together 'for the sake of (fill in the blank).' A relationship based on pretense almost always fails.

No pretense here

I'm not sure why, but Friday evenings seem to bring out Jacqueline's impulsivity. She has this way of casually mentioning things that often leave my ego flummoxed if not crushed. Let me give you an example. One such night we were reminiscing about a four-day music festival we attended several years prior. She recalled looking at me during a live performance and thinking how my face was so handsome. Just as my chest was heaving skyward, she then wondered aloud why she hadn't recognized this earlier in our relationship. This prompted me to ask my first stupid (and ego-driven) follow-up question:

"Well, did you not find my face attractive before?"

"I loved your eyes and your mouth!" she said.

"Okay... but what about my whole face?"

"Um... no—but I do now!"

"Ouch!" I thought. *"What the hell?!"*

Though it took almost an hour for my ego to nurse its wounds, I made important insights thanks to that exchange. I realized that Jacqueline's willingness to be authentic is a refreshing departure from my previous relationships. Sure, her forthrightness hurt my ego, but it also bolstered my confidence in knowing I can always count on her to be honest and authentic with me. Once I recovered, it was clear my fears were unwarranted since Jacqueline would never have a mate she found unattractive.

Tangentially, this episode also reminded me that the longer we are a couple, the more beautiful and attractive we both appear to each other. Even after years together, I am often overwhelmed by her beauty, inside and out, and I know she feels the same about me.

I was just being honest

Because English is not my first language (I only started speaking it about fifteen years ago), I have a theory. I notice that some of my words don't land the way I intend. Because of this, often when I say something, the recipient receives it negatively, or has their feelings hurt. Sometimes it gets me into big trouble. I just say what's on my mind without considering the other's feelings. Furthermore, my brain doesn't archive what words mean in different contexts. It surprises and even shocks people when I use certain descriptive words that seem provocative to them.

How this applies to the ego-crushing story above is that my habit of saying what's in my head, driven by how I feel, comes easy for me. I'm unabashedly honest in my statements. Although it has taken Michael some getting used to, I believe it has been a blessing to our relationship. What I said about my initial impression of his attractiveness was not an attempt to hurt him. Every woman is acutely aware of the fragility of her mate's ego. Although I am aware, it still doesn't stop me from speaking my mind.

Most unsatisfactory relationships are due to poor communication, which leads to misunderstandings. These worsen when either partner is unsure of what they want. This can lead to using sex as a substitute for intimacy and a defense against closeness.

My bluntness is a part of who I am: a woman with limitless potential for pleasure. I'm no longer in my childbearing years, instinctively fearing abandonment. So I say what I want when I want to, although I am learning that nuance matters. If I don't or can't tell my man what works for me in a gentle and loving way, shame on me!

Eliminating or greatly reducing pretense from your relationship is very straightforward, yet challenging. It requires a total commitment to authenticity and vulnerability from each partner. This is a commitment made easier by accepting that you are not your ego.

Chapter 16

ELIMINATING DRAMA

Drama, drama, drama

We live in a society where drama often forms the backdrop of our day-to-day lives. It shows up as events, life changes, cultural shifts and personal conflict. The implication is that anything worth paying attention to must be big or dramatic. Yet drama is what you want to avoid when building long-term, fulfilling relationships. It is a foundation made of shifting sands that will never support the vicissitudes of intimate relationships. From a healing perspective, drama is also the last thing a survivor needs in their life.

I suspect drama makes people feel more alive, which explains why so many crave it. The subtext seems to be that *you are not really living unless you have dramatic experiences all the time.* Clearly, drama can be highly addictive. Its siren song beckons us to a blissful, distraction largely to escape personal responsibility. Drama is also a way to avoid being Present.

Starve drama

An effective way to reduce drama in your relationship is to practice being a dispassionate observer in a state of Presence. This means being aware of being aware. Imagine viewing a movie of your life as you live it. You, the 'Observer', are watching, not reacting. An Observer does not judge whether things are 'good' or 'bad', they just *observe*. So, the next time tension arises around who forgot to run the dishwasher or take out the trash, step away, become present and just witness what happens instead of reacting. This removes much of the oxygen drama needs to thrive. The practice of being an Observer will also quiet your mind's drama-making machine. Once you are able to create your quiet port in the storm of life, you will notice that your partner and others will find you more attractive.

The next step is *selflessness*, which can be difficult in today's me-centric society. Selflessness means having no agenda other than to serve with no desire for reciprocation. It is barren soil for drama to take root. Keep in mind however, it's easy to act 'selflessly' for selfish reasons. High-functioning sociopaths and narcissists are adept at doing this, but it rarely ends well.

Little acts of selfless giving will go a long way to reduce drama and its impact. Here are a few simple things you can do to help end the drama within your relationship:

♡ **Open doors for her** – most women appreciate this more than you know, even if they don't say so.

♡ **Tell him how much you appreciate what he does for you** – men respond to this like you wouldn't believe.

♡ **Surprise her with a little gift** – it's not the size or cost that matters, it's the thought behind it, absent of expectation, that makes all the difference.

♡ **Give him a back-rub** – men love being touched in a nurturing way, especially if they don't expect it.

♡ **When you make love, focus on giving rather than receiving** – this alone will take your intimacy to new levels and your 'Drama Quotient' to near zero.

Practice non-drama

Drama is easy, sometimes even fun. It happens with no practice or effort, which explains its prevalence. Being present and acting selflessly will eliminate most drama from your relationship. It's like choosing between a Disneyland vacation and taking a contemplative walk in nature. One may be more exciting in the short run, but the other will serve you and your relationship for a lifetime.

Chapter 17

RELATIONSHIPS ON AUTOPILOT

Some of our strongest survival traits is our desire and ability to learn new things. Whenever we learn a new skill, we start out as consciously *incompetent*. This means we are painfully aware of our ineptitude. The more we practice, the better we become, until we reach the point of being conscious of our competence. High competence at this stage however, still requires being nearly 100% focused.

If we continue beyond that, we may reach the most sought after level of proficiency: *unconsciously competent*. This means that we don't have to think of what we're doing to do it well. This is when autopilot takes the helm. While mastery of any process or skill takes time, often years, Presence can happen in an instant because it's a state of *being*, not a process of doing.

Presence vs. doing

A while back, Jacqueline and I had an interesting exchange. She was stressing how novelty and new experiences can keep things fresh and exciting within a relationship. After pondering this a bit, I responded with, *"You know, even the pursuit of novelty can become a means to avoid being present."*

Consider the possibility that any 'doing' designed to instill newness and excitement into your relationship can become routine if not done in a state of Presence. All too often, couples fall into the trap of using activity as a distraction. The urge to do things together then becomes a way to avoid addressing old wounds: wounds that cannot hide while both partners are present for each other.

Autopilot is the antithesis of Presence. A state of Presence also means a willingness to face uncertainties. When you are present for each other, you experience the unfolding moment and are not attempting to anticipate the future. This is something our older, survival-imperative, lizard brains do not compute. Yet, accepting 'not knowing' allows incredible possibilities and breakthroughs to occur.

Here's Jacqueline's take on the need for novel activities to keep things fresh...

Why I was being emphatic

My adventurous spirit, as well as my love of learning and doing new things was what caused me to be so emphatic with Michael; I knew how easily relationships could slip into routine. I work hard, as does Michael, to keep things as fresh as they can be. It is Michael's nature to over-think things occasionally. So, of course, he had to be the devil's advocate when we were talking about ways to keep the relationship fresh. It is true, sometimes the effort to keep things fresh devolves into a series of doing new things while losing the preciousness of just 'being' together. This relationship means everything to me, and I will continue to work at it with all my might.

Routine: autopilot's path of choice

Routines are little processes we use to make our life easier, hassle-free, and less bothered by the scariest of all monsters: uncertainty.

Consider your intimate relationship for a moment and be candid. Where has routine already shown its face? Perhaps you and your partner saw the first signs and took steps to make your relationship more interesting and novel. If so, you may have fallen into the trap of using activities to give spice to your relationship. This approach is simply not sustainable.

We contend that no amount of *doing* can ever be enough for the long-term health and survival of an intimate relationship. It requires the *discipline* of Presence. Make no mistake, maintaining Presence is a discipline—one that can never go on autopilot, lest it vanish.

If you think of your most significant, intimate relationship as a work of art, you will see that it requires the same embracing of the unknown and the uncertain as any other creative endeavor. Only then will the full beauty of your mutual creation blossom and reveal itself. When you and your partner are present for each other, your relationship is no longer driving mindlessly down the road of mediocrity. Instead, it becomes the most exciting and exhilarating adventure of your lives. An adventure you can experience right now.

For example, every time Jacqueline and I go hiking, we are present for each other and the beauty of nature, which makes this a sacred experience. When we eat, we first hold hands and give gratitude for the abundance and deliciousness of the meal. When we kiss, we are so present that all outside thoughts cease, and our Beings seem to merge at the touch of our lips. Even something as simple as holding hands, for us, is a state of deep connection reflected in the acute awareness of our touch. Our mutual Presence in the bedroom prevents routine from diminishing our experience, and invites the extraordinary sexual intimacy we consistently enjoy.

Breaking the routine

You know how your car has warning lights, indicating something is or about to go wrong? Well, relationships have them, too. If you and your partner are no longer thrilled just by the sight of each other, that my friend, is a relationship warning light.

The quickest way to break routine that kills the thrill is to practice being present. You can start by sitting quietly together holding hands while avoiding the urge to fill the space with idle chatter or other forms of distraction. Notice how your Heart and body respond to being present for your significant other.

At first, you may experience discomfort as your quieted minds have nothing to distract them. However, your persistence will yield ample rewards. By staying with it, each of you will sense the deep calm and acceptance that comes with this space. Spontaneous ideas for new and interesting adventures may arise within this state of Presence. If so, consider it a bonus. The real payoff is sharing the uncertainty of the moment with your partner. Presence is the only state where routine cannot exist, and it is sure to raise your relationship to ever-greater heights of fulfillment.

Chapter 18

SLOWING DOWN

Just passing through

A few years ago, I hiked 200 breathtaking miles of the John Muir Trail with a group of friends. We were enjoying the stunningly beautiful vistas at the leisurely pace of 15 miles a day. One evening, as we were settling in for a well-deserved sleep, a tall, gaunt fellow came trotting up to our campsite, asking if we had any leftover food. He explained that he had just completed 70 miles of the trail *that same day*, and was getting hungry. He had obviously made distance a priority over provisions.

As he jogged away, one of my hiking buddies observed: *"It's like that guy is running through the Louvre."* In that man's quest for bragging rights, he had given up the most stunning aspects of the journey: exquisite beauty you can only witness when you slow down to take it all in.

Unfortunately, many of us are like that trail runner: on an obsessive ever-accelerating drive forward, making everything around us a veritable blur. Do you ever wonder why we are so hurried? It's as if this need for speed has become our raison d'être.

Caution: construction zone ahead

If you live anywhere near a city, ongoing road construction is a way of life. It's an annoyance and hurdle one must pass to reach the intended destination. When you travel down the road of life with your significant other however, these 'construction zones' are far more important than any journey's end. To ignore the impetus to slow down invites problems and lost opportunities for growth. Jacqueline and I have seen too many couples who are so active with their doing, they miss the most beautiful and transformative aspect of their relationship: simply *being* together.

Like our modern-day roads, relationships need to grow and occasionally repair to carry their tremendous loads: the naturally-occurring problems of sharing one's life with another. This is especially true when you consider how fast things are changing in our world.

This makes sense, right? But, how many couples do you know who take time to grow their relationship within the quiet solitude of no outside distractions? How many couples take notice of any cracks or potholes that may have formed and work together to fix them?

What slowing down looks like

There are many opportunities for slowing down to grow your relationship—and there are many ways to do it. When you meet or say goodbye to your partner, become present and take a moment to really see them. A practice Jacqueline and I often do is to acknowledge each other and seal it with a light, prolonged brush of our lips. It's nearly impossible to not be present when doing this. Conversely, the one thing we avoid is allowing distraction while together. This one practice alone will make a huge difference in most relationships.

Granted, there are times when our relationship does require upkeep. Our approach is straightforward. We insist on total authenticity in how we show up, what we are feeling, and in the careful choice of our words. We do this knowing any charges that may result are just the protestations of our respective egos.

The high cost of going too fast

In most areas of the U.S., if you receive a traffic ticket in a construction zone, the fines are double—and for good reason. It's far more dangerous for people and property to break traffic laws where road work is underway. The same goes for your relationship. If you don't slow down and pay full attention for periodic growth and maintenance, the penalty can be steep and painful.

The only difference is, instead of an embarrassing hit to your bank account and driving record, you could end up in a relationship that no longer serves either of you—or worse, without a relationship entirely.

Chapter 19

21ST CENTURY SOMA

In our work with couples, we've found that nothing suffocates intimacy more insidiously than distraction. Whenever Jacqueline and I are having dinner in a restaurant, we see couples who are supposedly there to enjoy each other's company, yet they insist on spending most of their meal buried in their smartphones. This is the 'new normal' that inhibits the intimacy most couples seek.

In Aldous Huxley's dystopian novel, *Brave New World* published in 1932, all citizens took a drug called Soma. Soma pacified the populace and provided pleasure, which made them numb to their authoritarian government's tight control.

Distraction is the 21st century Soma, placating our populace in much the same way. It shows up as entertainment, news, work, magazines, disconnected sex, food, alcohol, legal and illegal drugs, and the most prevalent of all, digital media. In this scenario, ego plays the part of the dark authoritarian government, seeking to control every aspect of our lives.

Whatever the source, distraction is about escaping the moment. It is a way of avoiding the discomfort that sometimes occurs with being present. Distraction lets our minds take over our lives at the expense of our Hearts. True intimacy requires real connection with other human beings, and real connection can only come from our Hearts, never our heads.

Slow death by distraction

Distraction has nasty side effects, including feelings of disconnection, depression, broken relationships, loss of passion or purpose, and an overall sense of being dead inside. Just like the fictional Soma, distraction placates and numbs us, turning the population into 'sheeple.' The most hopeful aspect of this addiction is the dim awareness that something significant is missing from our lives. Most human beings long for true connection with others. This longing is a lifeline that can connect us back to deep, Heart-centered intimacy with one another. Connection can guide us back to aliveness unless we continue to allow endless daily distractions.

The joy of being alive

Being joyously alive requires the willingness to experience *everything*, including the full spectrum of emotions, wonderful or otherwise. It requires listening to, as well as trusting one's Heart. It necessitates openness and vulnerability to the Hearts of others. Most importantly, it requires the courage to embrace the unknown, and the will to charge forward despite whatever fear may arise. No screen or distraction can compete with the profound rewards of living this way.

How to break the distraction habit

Here are several ways you can break free and recover from this relationship-damaging addiction:

- ♡ **Turn off your digital devices when with others** – use the off switch (that's its purpose).

- ♡ **Stop following the news** – most of what you see has no practical use, and most of it is negative.

- ♡ **Stop viewing TV** – living vicariously through entertainment will never be an adequate substitute for living life to the fullest.

- ♡ **Spend time in nature** – exercise, breathe fresh air, and allow Mother Nature to help you reconnect with everything and everyone around you.

- ♡ **Eat mindfully** – ask yourself why you are eating what you put into your mouth. If it's just to make you feel better, chances are it's just another distraction.

- ♡ **Practice gratitude** – when you express gratitude for *everything*, including life's challenges, you will experience each moment with joy.

- ♡ **Embrace uncertainty** – with the ability to sit with uncertainty, you gain discovery and wisdom.

- ♡ **Face your fears** – fears addressed head-on are far less potent than those we try to avoid.

- ♡ **Trust your Heart** – allow your Heart to be the captain of your fate, while your head acts as its faithful servant.

- ♡ **Practice being present** – don't get caught up in the story of your life. Practice watching your life unfold through the eyes of an Observer.

In a culture that bombards us with countless distractions, true intimacy requires the fierce determination to stay present. This is particularly true if you face the challenges of cancer. As you commit to kick the habit of distraction, you will soon notice the rewards of a vastly richer life and a deeper connection with the people you love.

However, our egos aren't going anywhere. This means we will always struggle with being present and are susceptible to falling back into the clutches of relationship-damaging distraction. Fortunately, we each have a choice: to accept the lulling sleep of distraction, or consciously strive to wake up and live free.

SECTION 3

Achieving Extraordinary Sexual Intimacy

*"If infatuation is madness,
then I want to be crazy."*

~ RUMI

Sex is a BIG deal, especially for committed couples who face the prospect of losing it or having it diminished due to cancer. Within this section, you will discover many ways to experience fulfilling sexual intimacy—as long as you pursue this material with open minds, creativity and a mutual sense of adventure.

The problem with the word 'sex' is its many definitions, depending upon who you ask. One can experience sex on a multitude of levels. There is the strictly physical act involving various forms of genital stimulation that can be very pleasurable and often leads to climactic release. Most couples that share physical attraction can experience this. The next level is when the sex act is only a part of a deeper, Heart-centered connection beyond just the physical. We call this sexual intimacy because the sex is only part of the connection. This elevated form of sexual experience is what we will focus on next.

If you and your partner open yourselves to the possibilities shared within the following chapters, you will discover an exciting new world of sexual intimacy waiting just for you, regardless of cancer's unwelcome visit to your life.

NOTE: This promise holds only if you have embarked on your journey to enhance your emotional intimacy as covered in the previous section. Without this, all bets are off.

Chapter 20

PRESENCE IS THE NEW PERFORMANCE

Have erectile dysfunction? Celebrate!

You read it right. Many women we've interviewed said the best lovers they've ever had were men with E.D. There are sound reasons for this unexpected accolade. Once you see what they are, your ideas about what constitutes fulfilling sexual intimacy may change forever.

E.D. - A woman's dream

In most cultures, the male potency imperative is so strong that I've had men tell me they *prefer death* to losing their erectile function. Even a temporary bout of E.D. is enough to send most men into a self-loathing funk followed by frantic calls to their doctors for erectile aid prescriptions. Men often view sexual performance in terms of: *equipment* (how big and hard), *stamina* (how long they can keep thrusting away) and, *how much they can drive their partner crazy with both*. Unfortunately, too many men buy into these myths. Mutually fulfilling sexual intimacy has *nothing* to do with performance. In fact, we have found the focus on performance is what *kills* great sex.

In a world overloaded with pharmaceutical advertising and porn revolving around men who can stay hard for hours, this anti-performance notion can seem foreign. When you replace performance with Presence, you open the door to a world of sexual intimacy beyond your wildest dreams.

Some women may accept these performance myths because they think this will please their man. When women *honestly* share what they most enjoy in the bedroom, it rarely matches the acrobatic stunts found in porn flicks. Don't believe me? Talk to several women and invite them to be candid.

Ask them what they want most. I'm sure you'll hear the theme of greater connection or Presence. Women want their men to be right there with them, playing and connecting in the moment—not attempting to achieve sexual athleticism. Women, in general, intuitively know performance is goal-oriented *doing*, while Presence is a space of goalless connection that may not involve any 'doing' whatsoever. When you are intimate with someone who is present, they accept you for who you are and you experience the warmth of their deep connection.

A man's perspective

When guys get a hard-on, we experience a visceral urge to use our penis and use it *now*. This tends to make sex very penile-centric. While this is perfect for making babies, it's rarely satisfying for sexual intimacy.

When men lose their ability to get erect, they also lose the sense of urgency that comes with it. If the man, so affected, can separate his sense of manhood from his erectile function, it opens him and his partner to other ways of being exquisitely intimate. This shift in paradigm means he is likely to slow down and be more present for his partner, perhaps in ways he never considered.

The easiest way to achieve Presence in the bedroom is expressing vulnerability, which means opening your Heart and being willing to feel everything. Our culture often views vulnerability as a weakness. However, if great sex is your destination, Presence is your vehicle and vulnerability is the key to the ignition. Just relax and put performance aside. Take a few calming breaths, and *be* with your partner without any expectations.

Men, invite your partner to share what works for her. Then, tell her that your sole focus is to please her in the way she wants. Reassure her, and ask her to receive and enjoy your love without concern for climaxing. When you create this safe, intimate space, you free her up to express her full sensuality.

A woman's perspective

A man's E.D. can negatively impact his female partner regardless of its cause. Women often misinterpret their man's flaccid response as a sign that he no longer finds her desirable...

> Many female partners of cancer survivors are in a state of perpetual insecurity. When their man experiences E.D., they often blame themselves. This leaves them at a disadvantage to deal with their relationship's sexual issues. You need to dig deep inside to discover the courageous and sexually curious part of yourself. This allows you to take charge of the situation for the benefit of your relationship.
>
> Once you become a conscious person, you return to your true essence: your Heart. This will allow you to be authentic and vulnerable for your intimate relationship. This is so important for your partner's struggle with this issue.
>
> The next step is to be in touch with your sexuality. Embrace the fact you are a sexual being and release any resistance to feeling sexy. There is no shame in wanting to seek physical pleasure in terms of what works for both of you. I see these womanly gifts from Nature as my birthright. You should too.
>
> When your man is less than confident about his ability to please you, that is the time for you to rediscover your sexual potential. Tactfully express how you feel so you don't further harm his already bruised self-esteem. True intimacy is a process in which each individual expresses important self-

relevant feelings and information to each other. As a result of sharing my wants and desires, and having Michael please me accordingly, I can't help to feel understood, validated and cared for. It makes our relationship resilient, promoting adaptation to life challenges when couples are coping with cancer. So, be the goddess and gently guide him toward new ways of pleasuring you he probably didn't know were possible.

Just to prove what I'm saying is true, Michael interviewed a forty-year-old woman who said her previous boyfriend had a temporary bout of impotence. Thanks to that, he became the world's greatest and most considerate lover. Then, when his function returned, in her words: *"He became a dick again, looking for other places to put it!"* Which explains why he is her previous boyfriend.

Age of Wisdom

Jacqueline and I have observed that a woman's age can have a big impact on how she wants and expresses intimacy. Generally, women of childbearing years put a much higher premium on sexual intercourse than others. This makes total sense within the context of nature's procreative imperative.

Once a woman approaches menopause, her desire for penetrative sex can wane. However, don't assume this means she wants less sex. It is *how* she wants to experience sexual intimacy that can differ greatly from her younger 'rip the clothes off' stage. Again, we base these observations on our own experience and on that of post-menopausal woman we have interviewed. There are always exceptions.

Under these circumstances, it is easy to imagine how a man with full impotence can be a blessing to his partner. Mutual acceptance of his loss of erectile function becomes an invitation to explore other paths of satisfying sexual fulfillment.

A woman's work

Should you ever learn that your man can no longer perform in the usual way, even temporarily, it is your cue to help him. First, reassure him that you love and find him as attractive and sexy as ever. Then, become his 'intimacy coach' by sharing the ways he can please you that *don't* require an erect penis. Remember, genuinely pleasing his partner is the greatest reward for a man who cares deeply for her. With your courage to help him with this, your mutual fulfillment and his confidence will soar.

The Last Word

Never allow the word 'performance' to enter your bedroom. Instead, replace it with Presence. This means making love without distractions, judgments or expectations. Again, if your guy has an issue with getting it up, see it as an invitation to explore other ways to be intimate. I assure you, with a little practice and a playful sense of adventure, you will find much to celebrate indeed.

Chapter 21

A NEW PARADIGM FOR MAKING LOVE

Just sex

We live in an over-sexualized society where anyone with an Internet connection can watch two (or more) people fornicating in every imaginable way (and some, well... *unimaginable* ways). It seems that our cultural narrative often defines 'making love' as just having sex.

The question is, how many of us truly equate having sex with making love? If making love is merely the physical act, then the 'making' part plays the dominant, if not exclusive, role. I suspect many feel there must be something deeper, more intimate, than the physical act, to deserve the tender moniker of 'making love.'

In my earlier years, sex and making love were no different for me—and most often, rather unsatisfying for all involved. Losing my ability to have an erection was an unexpected invitation to discover other ways of being intimate, including ways beyond the physical. By accepting that invitation, Jacqueline and I discovered the 'space' we create during intimacy is more important than what we do with or to each other.

Different ways, different places

A good friend of ours shared how she and her husband first 'made love' on the dance floor at a local bar. She went on to say how their every move conveyed a deep sense of mutual intimate giving that describes a much higher form of *making love*. This caused me to realize that so many couples have sex, but rarely make love. That's when it occurred that the notion of what it means to make love is worth re-examining.

Jacqueline and I have the same experience as our connubial, happy-footed friends. Anytime we walk, sit together or hold hands, we are making love. Most of the time, when we kiss, we are making love. When we lay together and listen to each other's hearts beat, we are making love. We've made love at the movies, while eating ice cream, walking on the beach or enjoying a concert. From this perspective, our lovemaking never stops. For us, making love is the selfless act of giving and receiving mutual connection, awareness and touch. From this perspective, making love requires neither a bed nor functioning body parts.

One time, we made beautiful love while staring into each other's eyes and synchronizing our breathing. That instance caused my entire body to shudder uncontrollably with pleasure, despite the fact that we weren't touching (section 4 of the book covers this unique, intimate experience in much greater detail).

When we climax, it is only one aspect of our lovemaking experience. That singular result never defines sexual intimacy for us. When the physical part ends, we are still making love as we lie in each other's arms, savoring our intimate connection. Thus, our sexual intimacy is enhanced beyond description.

So, next time you and your partner prepare to make love, consider what that means for your relationship. By incorporating this richer paradigm, your experience of intimacy will likely attain significant new highs. This is a repeatable and profound intimate experience of which no cancer, scars or impaired body function can ever deprive you.

Chapter 22

THE ECSTASY OF DELAYED GRATIFICATION

Based upon our own experience, it has become clear to Jacqueline and I that there are *no limits* to the depth and breadth of a woman's sexual and sensual capacity. Studies by famed sex researchers, Masters and Johnson, further corroborate this. They found some women can experience *50* separate orgasms during a single session of arousal. It almost makes you feel sorry for men whose experience of sexual peaking consists of a few minutes of thrusting, ending in a final grunt typically followed by rolling over to go to sleep.

However, there is no need for envy. We men can create the space that allows for the full blossoming of our woman's sexual experience. But this space can exist only when the man delays (not forgoes) his own gratification by *slowing down* to please her *first* in the way she prefers. By doing so, the man receives the greatest intimate reward of all, knowing he *genuinely* satisfied her like no other.

Thanks to this one simple shift in your sexual play, you become *the world's greatest lover* in her eyes. By delaying your gratification, you will see your sexual intimacy and overall relationship grow stronger and more fulfilling.

Why are men and women so different?

Nature wired us guys for one thing, sexually—to spread our seed as far, wide and often as possible. This is the reason we can be madly in love with our mate, but still steal glances of a cute gal walking nearby. It's why we have such a sense of urgency when we have an erection. This can generate a desperate need to seek release from its incessant yearnings, sometimes throwing caution and good sense to the wind. The reason for this wiring is straightforward: to populate our planet quickly and effectively. Our collective survival once depended upon it. But now that we have achieved that existential goal, that same wiring impedes many committed couples from achieving the deepest levels of sexual intimacy available to them.

This is a topic that elicits strong opinions from many women. With this in mind, here is Jacqueline's perspective on male sexual wiring...

I want to explain the blunt truth about male sexual behavior that sometimes gets misconstrued in the feminist dialog. When aroused, the urge to penetrate can seem physically overwhelming for healthy men. The question is: How much does testosterone control male sexual behavior? Almost entirely!

Women who've become cynical about men's motives have frequently claimed a man's brain is between their legs. To be more specific, you will find the male brain within the testes— their primary 'testosterone factory.' Aside from any confounding psychological factors, what primarily determines a man's sexual appetite is pure and simple: the amount of testosterone (T) in his system. If his T-levels are very high, there's greater potential for him to objectify, demean, or exploit the opposite sex.

Generally, how much testosterone we produce determines our sex drive. This is true for both sexes, although on average, men secrete at least ten times as much of this hormone as women[9]. While it's true that for women, a little testosterone goes a long way, it appears that men, in general, exhibit a stronger,

9 https://www.psychologytoday.com/blog/evolution-the-self/200904/the-testosterone-curse-part-1

more irrepressible sex drive than women.

Estrogen is the primary female sex hormone. It promotes the growth and health of the female reproductive organs and keeps the vagina moisturized, elastic, and well supplied with blood. Estrogen levels often decline during menopause, though this varies from woman to woman. Sometimes there can be more estrogen present during menopause than prior[10].

The differences between men and women show up in every corner of our relationships. Since we talk so much about authenticity, let's be honest about who we are as women and men. Men want sex, and if heterosexual, they want it from us.

However, this doesn't mean we women have to resign ourselves to do 'our duty' every time our partner has the urge. Since we are conscious beings, we can rise above innate instincts, and through care and authentic communication, guide our men to what works best for both.

A sensitive lover?

In the past, I fancied myself a sensitive and considerate lover. However, the primal urgency associated with an erection was always lurking around the corner and had significant (sometimes negative) influence on my lovemaking. In the immortal words of the late Robin Williams: *"God gave men a brain and a penis but only enough blood to run one at a time."* This is so true—at least it was for me before cancer-induced impotence. Prior to that, when I had erections, I just wanted to have sex—*period*. This did not always lead to the greatest fulfillment of my partners.

Prior to my chemical castration treatments, I still had a strong libido, but the visceral urge associated with an erection was no longer there. This allowed me to slow down for Jacqueline and please her

---

10 https://www.menopause.org/for-women/sexual-health-menopause-online/changes-at-midlife/changes-in-hormone-levels

first, in the way she wanted, before she reciprocated.

A British University study[11] showed that about 87% of women vocalize (i.e. moan) during intercourse primarily to boost their man's self-esteem and to speed things along. These lusty exhortations are not what most men interpret them to be: *"OMG, I LOVE IT when you pound me like a jackhammer!"* For many, the reality is more like: *"I want you to feel good as a lover, but let's just get this over with."*

Sadly, most women are reticent to share how and what they want during physical intimacy. This is mostly out of fear of abandonment and/or hurting their partner's feelings. This misinformed practice can create confusion and disconnect as to the reality of the intimacy they prefer.

When I slow down, Jacqueline warms up

Here is what Jacqueline and I do, which results in exquisite and unhurried lovemaking that can last for hours. Every woman will have her own preferences; we are just sharing what works for us:

- ♡ **Nurturing shower** – we start by taking turns scrubbing each other with a loofah, as a way to relax and get present for our impending intimacy. It is a tender expression of our mutual nurturing. Jacqueline is the first recipient as per my 'ladies first' rule.

- ♡ **Stress relieving massage** – we give each other a full-body, deep-tissue massage, using a high-quality massage oil. Prior to starting, I ask Jacqueline where she would like me to focus. After hearing the part of her body that requires the most attention, I massage her accordingly. Often, most of her stress is centered in her neck, shoulders and upper back, so I typically there. Here is the full massage sequence we use most of the time:

---

11 https://www.ncbi.nlm.nih.gov/pubmed/20480220

As she lays face-down—

> Neck, shoulders, upper back
>
> Lower back, buttocks
>
> Back of her legs

As she lays face-up—

> Upper back, neck, shoulders and scalp
>
> Arms
>
> Hands (I take extra time on her hands—it can be a relaxing and sensual practice that she feels in other areas of her body)
>
> Feet (these can be some of the most sensitive and sensual parts of the body)
>
> Top of her legs
>
> Stomach
>
> Breasts
>
> Pubic area (with little if any touching of her genitals)

Jacqueline and I are not professional masseuses nor have we received any formal training. We listen with our ears, feel with our hands and use our intuition to give the most nurturing massage we can while being fully present. It's not about 'doing it right.' Instead, the very act creates the enhanced sense of emotional connection through giving and receiving each other's touch. One thing to note at this point is that Jacqueline massages *me* first then I reciprocate. This is the only time we break our 'ladies first' rule. We do this because I want her to experience no interruption from being warmed up and aroused to receiving what comes next.

♡ **Intimate touching** – this transition into foreplay starts with a light caress of our fingertips along the skin and gentle kissing on the lips and other parts of our bodies.

After these steps, Jacqueline is typically ready for more overt sexual stimulation, which for us is oral. She finds that when I slowly and gently perform cunnilingus, it allows her to reach and stay at her fully aroused state over an extended period. We will cover this in much greater detail towards the end of this section.

Slowing, in this context, just serves to prolong and intensify both of our experiences. By delaying my gratification, I can take the requisite time to be present while giving to her. This consistently results in Jacqueline having a nearly endless series of climaxes until her desire for reciprocation exceeds the pleasure she is receiving.

When she returns the favor, the wait is well worth it. For any man willing to try, delaying his gratification to please his partner is its own considerable reward.

Lucky Me...

I found a man with severe erectile dysfunction, which helped make him coachable. As a self-confident and secure woman, I understand that Michael won't abandon me just because it takes time for my body to warm up and have orgasms. Women need to drop the old belief that their man will judge them if they need more time to build arousal. Some women also fear abandonment if they seem to know more about sex than their mate. Those fears may have been legitimate when you were in your 20s or 30s, but now, as a mature woman, you should be Commander-in-Chief in the bedroom. You come first. The 'waiting' should never be a deterrent. When we allow our men to be the source of our pleasure, it's his win as well. Most likely, he will feel he has scored big if you authentically climax. Of course, his release should please you as well.

Every woman should realize the utmost joy for men is to please his partner, genuinely. He should remember that each woman is unique. Even if your significant other has lots of experience in the bedroom, he doesn't automatically know your particular sexual preferences. You must communicate, in detail, what works for you. He wants and needs to understand how to get you there. That is assuming, of course, you want to climax. If you don't, that's okay too; he must respect that.

Allowing vs. making

Slowing down for Jacqueline has allowed me to create an inviting space where she will often climax many times. I don't stop until she asks, feels satiated or is on fire to reciprocate.

I never *make* Jacqueline climax. Instead, through a state of unwavering Presence, I give her the space to express uninhibited sensual potential. Now, this next part is extremely important. Creating a space that *allows* your female partner to climax is NOT the same as *making* her climax. Any attempt, or even implied expectation, to have your partner achieve orgasm, is the quickest way to quell that possibility and generate considerable performance anxiety.

She comes first

In his best-selling book, *She Comes First – The Thinking Man's Guide to Pleasuring a Woman*, author Ian Kerner, Ph.D., expounds the many reasons male-delayed gratification is crucial to maximizing the female's sexual response. He cites many scientific studies to support that contention.

Physiologically and psychologically, women differ from men on the time and means required for sexual arousal. This typically results in a more gradual sexual response profile. To ignore these differences and just plow ahead to satisfy erectile longings leaves much on the table in terms of sexual fulfillment and satisfaction for both parties.

Chapter 23

UNDRESSING FOR
INTIMATE SUCCESS

Slow, sensual and present

Many couples experience the frantic, lust-laced ripping-each-other's-clothes-off moments of unbridled passion during the early days of their relationship. Yes, this stage is exciting and breathtaking, but often, short-lived. This is a phase that eventually succumbs to a more subdued routine process where both of you arrive naked. Part of what drives this frenzied first stage of sexual entanglement is the novelty of exploring each other as new lovers. However, this newness fades eventually.

Jacqueline and I are constantly trying new things in our relationship. One intimate ritual we discovered is undressing each other in a slow, sensual way. We do this before we make love, before we take a shower, before retiring to bed, and as we change clothes before we go out. Most of the time however, we perform this ritual with no thought of it leading to sex. We do it for the mutual enjoyment and appreciation of our relationship, and always within the sensually fertile space of Presence.

We start out nose-to-nose as we gaze into each other's eyes. Then, we lightly caress each other's fully clothed bodies. Where we disrobe doesn't matter, how we disrobe doesn't matter—the only thing that matters is taking our time. We find that when we slowly remove a piece of the other's clothing, it builds an enormous amount of sensual energy between us. For me, just the feel of lifting Jacqueline's blouse, while it lightly rubs her exposed skin, can be almost overwhelming. If you are not mindful and present, this heightened state of arousal can easily turn into the wild shedding of clothing, which will break the spell.

Once we remove the first garments, we take a while to caress and kiss each other in the exposed areas. We follow this with soft, gentle kissing of our lips, barely allowing them to touch. We continue this undressing, caressing and kissing until we are standing nude. A sexy variation is looking in a large mirror as we disrobe. In these instances, our caressing is explorative and designed to ignite our sensual imaginations.

We understand some people are uncomfortable looking at their own or their partner's naked body. In this case, consider dimming the lights or turning them off. Let your imagination be your guide as your hands and lips explore each other in the darkness. Whether the lights are on or off, this can be a deeply connecting experience of heightened sensuality.

It doesn't always have to lead to sex

It is common for women to hesitate even kissing their male partner for fear he may misinterpret the action as a desire for sex, when she may only want connection. You might ask yourself, *why would a couple even bother with this ritual if they don't intend to follow it up with sex?* The answer is: *"Why not?"* Anything that rekindles passion (delayed or otherwise), and heightens mutual sensuality for you and your partner, is a habit worth doing.

Women, in particular, seem to appreciate these kinds of unexpected sensual experiences that don't always lead to sex. Jacqueline's thoughts on this are loud and clear...

> Men, can you hear me? Everything need not lead to sex. Men and women are starkly different. He wants sex, she wants relationship. He wants flesh, she wants love and companionship. As children, society teaches us to compete if you are a boy, and collaborate if you are a girl.
>
> If there was one thing that I wish all men understood, it's

that women don't require sexual intercourse to feel an intimate connection. For women, intimacy has many levels, and not just between the sheets.

While it may come as a surprise, women do not find pictures of nude men and male genitalia exciting. Porn and images of female genitalia however, easily excite men, because they spark their imaginations, helping them to fantasize about all the things they could do with the female body. Sex, for men, can be impersonal and release-centered. It's all about flesh, and it doesn't matter with whom. Nature organizes women's minds differently. We place relationships as a top priority, much different from the male mind, which prioritizes achievement at all cost. Men like to keep score of their sexual conquests, but for women, only connection counts.

Despite these divergent differences, having intimate relationships is still what most men and women desire. The problem is that we all fail to communicate or act appropriately based on what each of us *needs*. This is why this undressing exercise has significant value: it slows us down to play, with no endgame in mind.

For our male readers, we ask you to imagine the impact that this sensual undressing ritual might have on your relationship. You will be building an enormous bank account of trust, appreciation and emotional intimacy with your partner. When you do engage in sexual intimacy, you are likely to find it much more exciting and fulfilling—as will your partner. Don't let your busy schedules be an excuse for not regularly doing this beautiful reminder of what is truly important.

Chapter 24

SEXUAL GIVING

The ultimate male orgasm

As mentioned earlier, the first time Jacqueline and I made love, we spent hours experiencing deep connection, intimacy and exquisite pleasuring. Jacqueline climaxed multiple times, which gave me the confidence I could still be a 'man.' However, as excited as I was, and no matter how she tried to stimulate me, I could not release. In fact, I tried so hard that I got exertion headaches.

What surprised me was my lack of sexual frustration, despite my inability to climax. The truth is, I'd *never* felt so fulfilled. This response puzzled me because it was outside my previous sexual experiences. After many sexless years, I would typically be climbing the walls. Instead, I was basking in the deep glow of intimate satisfaction.

About a month and a half into our sexual intimacy, I stopped trying, and allowed myself to receive Jacqueline's loving *passively*, and enjoy the ride without expectations. That was the trick that enabled my brain to 'rewire,' causing me to experience my first orgasm with a woman in over 12 years. It was incredible and completely *different* from a typical male climax, or anything like I'd ever experienced. Prior to my cancer, I had no problem having explosive ejaculatory orgasms. However, compared to what happens now, there is no contest. I can only imagine that these pulsing waves of ecstasy are similar to what women experience during climax. I wouldn't trade this for anything, including getting my hard-on back.

Let me try my best to explain what happens:

As I start to peak, it originates within my entire pelvic region (not just my penis), as high-voltage waves of undulating pleasure that travel up through the femurs of both legs, all the way to my kneecaps. Its extraordinary power and duration causes me to scream nearly every time. Since then, my orgasms continue to grow stronger and longer lasting. However, I am hardly unique in this capacity. I've had other men who lost their ability to ejaculate contact me to say they had similar experiences. Think about it. This is *incredible* news for every man and their partner dealing with prostatectomy-induced impotence. This largely unknown capability is all due to the plasticity of our brains in rewiring how we experience sexual pleasure and release.

Not knowing what you don't know

When I attempt to explain this experience to men with unimpaired ejaculatory response, they usually give me a look that says: *"Bulls**t!"* or *"Good for you but I have no idea what the hell you are talking about."* The irony here is, this whole-body climax is much easier for non-ejaculatory impotent men to achieve than those who function normally. That's because the procreative male orgasmic response is so hard-wired into men it overwhelms any attempt to suppress it. I suspect this suppression is a minimum requirement for any man to experience this greatly enhanced sexual release. In terms of sexual epistemology, for the majority of our male population, this falls squarely within the realm of *you don't know what you don't know.*

Better than mind-blowing climaxes

Jacqueline and I openly discuss our intimate experiences, including respective preferences. We often ask each other the same question: *"If you had to give up one thing, the receiving or the giving, which would it be?"*

Without a hint of hesitation, we both say we'd give up the receiving, as long as we could continue to give. Stop for a moment and consider this within the context of the intense orgasms we each experience. When many couples become intimate, their primary focus is usually on how they can *receive* pleasure. What we have discovered is we derive our greatest pleasure from the ability to *give* to each other selflessly. Sexual giving, without conditions or expectations, consistently provides us the most intense, pleasurable and fulfilling intimate experiences.

The next time you make love, ask your partner what they want. Then be present as you accommodate their desires by giving with no attachment to the outcome. Pay attention to what happens to them, and what happens to *you*.

Chapter 25

TALK...NEVER TOO MUCH

Do tell

Jacqueline and I have observed that most women consistently do one thing that severely limits possibilities in the bedroom. Now, please don't shoot the messenger. We contend if women would stop this one behavior, it would open both partners to more fulfilling intimate experiences. It only requires a bit of courage to make this change.

By not being authentic about their sexual desires, women sabotage the potential for unlimited sexual intimacy, and set themselves up for frustration. Fortunately, you can take steps to avoid this.

Frustration to bliss

Women, here are fundamental principles about men that, when applied in the bedroom, will transform your sexual intimacy:

1. ***Men aren't mind readers*** – never assume that he can read your mind. This assumption only creates drama, confusion and frustration.

2. ***Men love variety in the bedroom*** – variety is not a bad thing... it's all about directing it so it works for both of you.

3. ***The greatest sexual fulfillment for a man is pleasing his partner*** – as a man, I have found that providing Jacqueline with an extraordinary sexual experience is its own reward—

one that is far greater than me just 'getting off.' However, women must be willing to tell their man what they prefer during sexual intimacy. Only then can he genuinely please his mate and experience the deep fulfillment of doing so.

NOTE TO MEN: be sure to listen and follow what she says—you will never regret doing so. If you don't, she may never trust you again with her desires.

Coach, don't tell

Ladies, at this point you can be your man's intimacy coach. Don't hold anything back. The number one thing to remember is to always reward him with authentic feedback when he does things right, and *gently* redirect him when he doesn't.

I think we can all agree that men's egos can be quite fragile regarding how you view their sexual 'performance.' So, a word of warning. If you tell your man, *"Ah Honey, what you're doing doesn't work for me, try this instead..."* you will trash his ego and likely cause a major rift in your relationship.

Now, consider *coaching* him this way (don't hesitate to use your own words): *"Honey, I so love it when you _____! I was thinking, how would you like to explore other ways to make love that may take our experience to even greater heights?"*

Let's examine what I did here. First, I complimented him on some aspect of our lovemaking. Pick something you can authentically praise. The next part is worded in a way that appeals to men's desire for sexual variety. This results in a strong, positive motivator to make love in the way you want.

By being honest in the bedroom, you are helping him to please you genuinely in a way that makes him feel wonderful too. Keep in mind however, it's all in the positioning.

I think I can safely speak for most men on this next point. If our partner said to us what Jacqueline suggested above, we would drool copiously as we endeavored to find out what new sexual surprises were in store.

It's ironic that we live in a culture where sex is everywhere, yet the vast majority of couples are struggling with less-than-fulfilling sexual intimacy. This is especially true as they mature. Changing that starts with absolute authenticity on the woman's part, as well as her partner's coachability. Once you start down that path, neither of you will look back.

As covered earlier in the book, women's sexual intimacy preferences can change with age. Therefore, it is important that women develop a habit of authentic communication about their sexual desires, especially as they shift over time. Otherwise, their partner will be unlikely to please them in the way they desire, which ends up serving no one.

Chapter 26

YOUR PARTNER'S SEXUAL RESPONSE PROFILE

Men and women are different. Aside from the obvious, the way men and women respond sexually tend to be worlds apart, which can cause a great deal of frustration in the bedroom. The difference between a ho-hum sexual experience and a transcendental one is understanding and adjusting to your partner's unique sexual response profile.

Sexual response profile

The sexual response profile is the way an individual *most effectively* progresses through their sexual response cycle, or phases of physiological arousal. This is generally different for each gender. Emphasis of 'most effectively' above implies the sexual response profile reflects the *optimum* way a person traverses through their arousal cycle.

Most women's sexual response profiles change as they age. For example, the time needed for sufficient arousal usually increases with age, especially when they are post-menopausal. They may also need different forms of sexual stimulation than they did during their childbearing years. Men, on the other hand, see subtle, nuanced changes in their sexual response profile. However, that can change significantly if the man has a reproductive cancer. My prostate cancer chemical castration therapy causes my warm-up period to be much longer than before, something that Jacqueline readily accommodates. By fully surrendering to her prolonged stimulus, I experience the most powerful and longest lasting full-body orgasms mentioned in an earlier chapter.

Matching her profile

What I share with you next results from my experience as an impotent man who has learned how to match or *harmonize* with his female partner's sexual response profile. Thanks to my impotence, I am much more coachable as a lover than I was previously. In listening to Jacqueline, I discovered that what worked for her and what I thought would work were two different things.

As men, we are designed for intercourse. While this may be lots of fun for us guys, it's not always conducive to having a sexually fulfilling experience from the female perspective. For example, like most women who are post-menopausal, Jacqueline takes much longer to warm up than I do. One of the biggest complaints we hear from women is that, by the time their guy issues his last grunt, she's barely getting started.

I am very fortunate that Jacqueline is not shy about sharing what she likes—including me taking more time for her optimal arousal. My impotence made this easier to accomplish since I don't have the urge most other men get when they are hard. This allows me to focus on taking my time to prepare and please her in the way she wants.

Sensuality unleashed

By matching Jacqueline's sexual response profile in this way, she ends up having the most incredible sensual experience. We have yet to find the limits of her sexual expression. This, and research done by others, has led us to the conclusion that women with a healthy sexual self-image have few, if any, bounds to their sensual expression. Imagine that possibility and what it means for your relationship.

Get more by giving

What this does for me as her lover goes beyond anything she could do for me in terms of reciprocation. The ability to provide her that experience is a far greater and more fulfilling form of connection than any release I could receive from her.

As men, we are easy to please sexually. However, there is a huge difference between getting off and being exquisitely fulfilled. I believe we are also hard-wired to receive deep satisfaction by giving it. As a result of matching her sexual response profile, I can attest that, having experienced her subsequent extraordinary sensuality, my level of sexual satisfaction has never been greater. That has become, and continues to be, its own reward beyond measure.

Chapter 27

NO MORE FAKING IT

Faking it is a symptom of people who are out of touch with their true desires. People who 'fake it' allow others to decide what they should want, or they settle for whatever they think they can get. It is about buying into the social conditioning that the real purpose of existence is to work at a meaningless job, engage in buying stuff that impresses, and acquire the newest gadgets in an effort to achieve a momentary feeling of satisfaction. We do this while digging ourselves into debt and distracting ourselves with mindless entertainment. Then, we get married, have children, and subject the kids to more or less of the same, which inevitably results in retiring and dying quietly with regrets.

The faking I cynically described crystallizes the issue of inauthenticity. Why is there so much sexual deception plaguing our relationships?

Many, if not most women, have an almost visceral fear they will disappoint their man if they don't react to him in the way he wants. This can cause a great deal of performance anxiety in women, which only makes it more difficult to experience genuinely what they've become so good at faking. Also, when she's faking it, he's pretending to buy it. This is a sad charade carried on by countless couples that will almost always lead to eventual disappointment and frustration within their relationship and perhaps even the end of it.

We already covered the woman's perspective of not enjoying sex when it's too fast, too hard and too immediate. Why don't men ask the necessary questions? Why do men convince themselves they satisfy their woman without probing further? When a man assumes he satisfies his woman, and never asks about it, he is essentially faking it too!

Fear of intimacy is a predictor of motivation for faking orgasm. Men and women who had difficulty in a past relationship are more likely to fake to avoid feeling insecure about themselves, or to end the sexual encounter.

Why this matters for men

Most men want their experience, as well as their mental and emotional states, to be understood by their partner. The faking can stop when women develop a better understanding of the real, intrinsic reward men seek, and men stop saying anything to get laid.

For men to engage in the hard work of change, the rewards must be automatic and visceral, independent of vague therapeutic concepts. They need to *feel* compelling reasons to change and, most importantly, incorporate new behaviors into their daily routine.

The primary motivation keeping men invested in loving relationships differs from what keeps women invested. The glue that keeps men (and males in social animal groups), bonded, is the instinct to protect. If you listen long enough to men talking about what it means to love, you'll notice they inextricably link providing protection with giving love. If men can't feel successful at protecting, they can't fully love. On some level, men also want authentic communication with their female partner. Sadly, too many women still haven't realized how important it is to overcome their fear of speaking up.

Having patience and understanding will make it easier to draw men out over the long run. To encourage more communication from your woman, don't make faces or act like your ego gets hurt when she shares authentically with you. Men, take the initiative and assure your woman you will not freak out if she voices her needs. Be clear that you won't judge her if she decides orgasms don't have to be the star of the show every time she has sex.

Chapter 28

AGING SEXUALLY

Bad news...

You know the joke, *"If you want sex, don't get married!"* Well, it's largely true... and it gets worse. According to an analysis of U.S. Census data[12], 36% of women in their 40s who currently live with a same-sex romantic partner, were previously in a heterosexual marriage. Among women in their 50s living with another woman, over 50% had left a straight marriage. This percentage jumps to 75% for those 60 or older. My take? As women age, their need for intimacy, and their preferred expression of it, can shift dramatically. This can lead to exploring the possibility of a same-sex relationship, despite their previous sexual orientation. Others prefer a sexless life over one with sex they no longer find enjoyable—whether as 'roommates' with their long-term partner or alone.

Good news...

It is possible to have your intimate life become better as you mature. In the Ladies Home Journal article, *Let's Talk About Sex (and Why I'd Rather Just Go to Sleep)*, CBS News Correspondent, Lee Woodruff said: *"To be honest, I can take sex or leave it, and mostly I'd rather leave it."* In a follow up video interview with CBS News chief medical correspondent, Dr. Jon LaPook, Mrs. Woodruff also shared how her husband of 25

---

12 These statistics were reported by a number of online publications ostensibly from the research of Dr. Gary Gates (retired) of the Williams Institute. The actual source report is not currently available due to Dr. Gates retirement.

years, Bob Woodruff (also a journalist), is 'ready for action', all the time. She admitted that sometimes she gives in to perform her 'wifely duty.' Of course, men can also sometimes feel an obligation to provide sex when they are not in the mood.

Faulty wiring

Again, biological and cultural wiring significantly impacts the way men and women are in the bedroom. To make babies, our wiring is perfect. However, most of us have evolved beyond the need to use sex as an exclusively procreative process. We also use it in an attempt to connect deeply with another human being. It is the conflict between seeking deep connection and the hard-wired imperative for procreation that causes many of the problems that occur for committed couples, especially as they age. In the early years of most relationships, intercourse is exciting and pleasurable to both partners. Thanks to their innate wiring, most women during their childbearing years desire intercourse regardless of their longing for children. However, as women mature, many see their sexual intimacy preferences shift. Emotional and non-sexual forms of intimacy become far more important. Intercourse becomes less desirable, and for many, painful.

Many mature women have concern that their partner no longer finds them attractive. These women have fears of being replaced by a 'newer model', whose sexual desires are more like their aging male partner. Age does not seem to impact men's sexual intimacy preferences in the same way as it does women. This comes from the observation that no matter the man's age, most still prefer penetrative sex.

This is where the breakdown occurs. As we have said, women are sometimes reluctant to share what they want in terms of sexual intimacy, fearing their mate may become hurt, angry, or worse—leave the relationship. Men remain clueless, disappointed and frustrated, not knowing why their partner of many years appears to no longer be interested in him.

Once the divide reaches a certain point, both partners become dissatisfied with their intimate life, despite still caring for each other and craving intimacy and connection. The problem is, they no longer know how to manifest it within the context of their respective age-related changes.

When that happens, one of the following often occurs:

a) **They both just settle for a sexless relationship** – they become roommates (often due to the cost and uncertainty involved in separation).

b) **She splits** – the woman either resigns herself to a single, sexless existence, or she risks seeking the quality of intimacy her Heart craves in another man or woman.

c) **He splits** – he seeks a woman (often younger), with whom he can enjoy sex, just like he always did.

The way back

These potential outcomes need not be the final fate for any long-term relationship. It is possible for couples to experience the most exciting and fulfilling physical intimacy of their relationship in their later years. This is particularly pertinent for those long-term couples who are also dealing with the challenges and stress of cancer. However, this requires that they both change their attitudes and behaviors.

It is incumbent upon women to communicate authentically what they want in terms of intimacy, especially as it changes over time. For men, it is crucial to listen and accommodate their mate's requests. Men must also realize that as women age, they take much longer to warm up to physical intimacy than they did in the early stages of their relationship.

This makes me wonder how different things could be for Lee and Bob Woodruff, and countless other middle-aged couples, if they approached their intimate needs this way. I suspect that Mrs. Woodruff would excitedly report on an entirely different experience. This would be due to her willingness to communicate authentically, and her husband's commitment to adapt to her changing needs and desires.

Male partners have the power to unlock the unlimited sexual potential of their women at any age, and reap extraordinary sexual fulfillment. It requires that they listen and tame their penile-centric urges.

Menopause, the lame excuse

I recently visited a friend in the mid-West. On all outward appearances, he is in a good marriage with an attractive wife in her early 40's. He shared with me that his wife was showing a much lower desire for sex. Her excuse: menopause. When I mentioned this to Jacqueline she matter-of-factly said, *"Oh, women just use that as an excuse."*

As you might expect, she has quite a bit more to share about this topic...

> When I said that to Michael, about our friend and his wife's excuse, I realized how serious this problem is. Our society appears to be experiencing a sexless marriage epidemic. Studies have demonstrated that not just older couples, but also many young, and otherwise healthy married people, are foregoing sex for long periods... and others have given it up altogether.

> The key to the way out of this conundrum is understanding that nature wires us to procreate. For younger women, there's an inborn imperative to want children. Luckily, I transcended this period, and emerged as a conscious human being for whom the urge for penetrative (i.e. procreative) sex has faded away. This new awareness about my sexuality harmoniously coincided with my desire to enjoy sex and intimacy on my own terms.

> The stories of women crying out publicly for help for their sex lives litter popular literature. For example, actress Patricia Heaton writes about it in her memoir, *Motherhood and Hollywood: How to get a job like mine.* There are others that are

more blatant, including books such as *Okay, So I Don't Have a Headache* by Cristina Ferrare and *I'm Not in the Mood: What every woman should know about improving her libido* by Judith Reichman. Another popular book that was a hit among Oprah Winfrey's crowd is *For Women Only: What you need to know about the inner lives of men* by Shaunti Feldhan. In this book, she lists techniques that married women use to avoid sex. From the age-old strategy of feigning sleep to the contemporary practice of taking on night-owl household projects.

Michael and I never worry about this issue, thanks to our undying commitment to authentic communication and being aware of our respective needs. We treat sex as one of our relationship maintenance activities. We address these needs by scheduling our lovemaking once a week. This has been a great strategy to not let our busy lives inhibit us from having extraordinary sexual intimacy every time.

At the start of our relationship, we lived separately and only spent weekends together, which was a great arrangement. Now, we live together, and find that maintaining separate bedrooms and sleeping together only on weekends is a miracle for our intimacy. This keeps the relationship exciting and avoids the relationship-deadening 'autopilot' syndrome. I never want to repeat the same recipe of my prior marriage, not this time. Michael and I truly treasure our relationship... and that's why we strive to stay away from old relationship templates that, based on divorce statistics, clearly don't work.

When you are not having sexual thoughts or feeling particularly sexy, push yourself to get started. Don't wait for your significant other to start things. Initiating something yourself can feel incredible! Men often respond positively to their mate's sexual prompting. Most often, I get in the mood because I'm thinking about the sublime climactic release that acts as a detox to shake off stress and connect me with my true essence. Consider making subtle or not-so-subtle movements to get you thinking about and, warming up to, sexual intimacy.

I love hot water on my body. Having Michael tenderly wash me in the shower makes me feel like I am in heaven. This also seems to trigger forces at work within my biology that signals me to just BE and receive his loving. The massage sessions we do together afterwards seal the deal and, two hours later, I'm so ready I can barely hold it together.

Jacqueline explained that menopause affected *how* she wanted to have sex, not her *desire*. Intercourse became quite uncomfortable for her, and prolonged thrusting rarely led to climax. Given that most men at any age prefer penetrative sex, and a majority of women hesitate to tell their partner what they want, you can see why menopause is the perfect excuse.

As women age, the desire for intimacy generally does not wane, yet their preferred expression of it often does. Physiologically, intercourse is not the most pleasurable way women can experience sex. For most women, direct clitoral stimulation trumps penetration. Yet men, in general, seem to have a difficult time understanding that what worked before (i.e. intercourse), is no longer appealing for their mate.

No to resignation, yes to authenticity

When I offered to help my friend, he said: *"Thanks, but that's just the way it is."* This is a difficult subject for most couples, due to many primal fears associated with our default Sexual Operating System. The danger here is that resignation turns into relationship-destroying resentment. Authentic communication prevents this resentment from taking root. Female partners need the fortitude to express sincerely what they want from her mate, especially if it changes over time. Male partners need to listen and do their best to comply. Now, before too many men reading this knee-jerk into a, *"Hey, what about my needs?!"* response, know this:

When you can *genuinely* please her, and she is no longer faking it or giving excuses, you will be one very happy camper. So, the next time you hear, *"Not tonight Honey because I _____..."*, treat it as an invitation to start an honest conversation about what she wants in the bedroom. Chances are, she will love and cherish you all that much more because you risked doing so.

Chapter 29

PHALLUS-CENTRIC FALLACY

I remember hearing a story about one fellow bragging up his new penile implant. When he showed it to his wife in all its upstanding glory, he didn't quite get the reaction he was hoping...

"Where do you think you're going to stick THAT?!"

Here's a related comment from a reader of one of my articles:

"At 64, the decline of my sexual prowess is noticeable. Rather than reach for the little blue pill, I discovered, as you have, the joys of giving pleasure. To me, the most erotic thing in the world is seeing, hearing and feeling my wife's sexual arousal. Wish I could have discovered this years ago. Hope your message reaches a young audience."

I receive many comments to my articles on sexual intimacy. They are all great indicators of the problems we try to address in our work.

Intercourse is okay, but...

In the beginning months of our intimate relationship, Jacqueline and I experimented with having intercourse—*all of one time.* This required a penile injection, since all the other erectile medications didn't work. I was willing to make my member a pin-cushion just to see if we were really missing anything.

Jacqueline helped me with the rather delicate and somewhat painful procedure. After about 15 minutes I had a significant erection, a condition I had not seen or felt in many months. From that perspective alone, it was very exciting. However, I also noticed how the old urges washed over me as my erection became more pronounced.

Now this next part is extremely important.

I was aware of my growing and visceral sense of urgency to engage in intercourse. Instead of allowing for our usual, gradual warm-up, which can take anywhere from 40 to 90 minutes, we plunged right in to this most common of sex acts. It lasted all of 10 or 15 minutes, ending with a typical ejaculatory-response orgasm—sans the ejaculate as I have no prostate. Not surprisingly, Jacqueline did not climax.

Did we find it pleasurable? Sure. Yet, it wasn't even remotely close to what we otherwise experience in terms of mutual sexual fulfillment. Our concern for how long I could stay hard, along with my visceral desire to penetrate right away, caused us to abridge our usual multi-hour lovemaking sessions. This left us both feeling quite empty. I remember looking into her eyes afterwards with a bit of sadness, saying, *"I will NEVER do that again."* The look on her face said: *"I agree, thank you…"* and we haven't, since. I will never again allow my visceral urges to take the place of our sacred and conscious lovemaking. This is yet another reason I am not interested whatsoever in regaining my erectile function.

A match made in heaven

As women, regardless of age, socioeconomic and cultural differences, we love the idea that the world doesn't revolve around the penis. That's a good thing!

When we look at the facts, at least 50% of men in the U.S. experience erectile dysfunction in their lifetime. Just like menopause symptoms and side effects, the medical community is quick to label E.D. as a 'pathology,' which makes it easy for the pharmaceutical industry to 'fix' it. Nearly 100% of women suffer the dramatic symptoms of menopause, which, ironically, leaves them desiring what an impotent man is best suited to give.

When Michael told me he was impotent five years ago, I didn't know what that would mean for us as a couple. At that moment, I sensed intuitively there were possibilities I wanted to explore. In my experience, when a penis was 'calling the shots,' it wasn't always my preferred form of intimacy.

What I've learned with Michael, is that men must create the space for their female partners to blossom sexually. Ladies, our sexuality is deep within us, but for most women, it needs gentle encouragement. The truth is most women can enjoy sex more as they grow older, even after menopause or a hysterectomy. After those events, we often feel freer to enjoy intimacy and sex absent fear of pregnancy or prudish guilt. It takes an evolved man to understand his role in creating that space for us. Michael is the only impotent man I have experienced. The insights we gained suggests all men with E.D. are particularly well-suited to provide the space we women need to enjoy sex at any age.

As we age, and our bodies change, we must adapt our view of these often-dreaded changes. We must consider these challenges a time to reconsider. Any important transition requires both physical and emotional adjustments. Once you and your partner master emotional intimacy, the techniques described in this book will open you to new possibilities. When you do as I have, you will find menopause and E.D. is indeed a match made in heaven.

What the ladies say

Here's yet another conversation that further speaks to our approach. A young man, Matthew, wrote in to comment about another article. He questioned why women needed men for sexual satisfaction at all when they can purchase any size or shape 'package' they want. Rebecca replied with this:

> *"Matthew, let me assure you that the intimacy and excitement that comes from being with a partner who is emotionally and physically present, is far, far greater than anything a woman could possibly buy at the store."*

Penis-centricity

Popular culture and the pharmaceutical industry would have us believe physical intimacy revolves around the penis. Unfortunately, buying into this myth can cause problems in the bedroom.

How men and women express sexual intimacy is a function of upbringing, experience and how informed/uninhibited they are about each other's sexuality. The other key element is their age. For women, it may be menopause and a changing body. Men also experience physical changes that can impact their potency, with or without cancer. With these changes, women often resort to distancing themselves from physical intimacy, while men reach for erectile aids to return to 'the way things were.'

Shutting down or using external aids intended to 'fix' our intimacy issues will never work. We can't emphasize this enough: as women age, their needs and ways of expressing physical intimacy will likely change. This doesn't mean they are no longer interested in sex; it's often quite the opposite.

At a later stage in their life, women view Presence, vulnerability, authenticity and open-Heartedness as far greater turn-ons than the 15-20 minutes of thrusting they used to experience.

Limited only by your imagination

What are other ways you can experience great sex besides intercourse or another form of penetration? Well…a little imagination and an adventurous spirit can help answer that. What works best for you and your partner may still be undiscovered territory. Explore your sexually intimate possibilities with the spirit of enthusiastic adventure-seekers by celebrating victories and laughing at faux pas.

In the next chapter, we will delve more explicitly into how Jacqueline and I experience extraordinary sexual intimacy, despite my cancer and her menopause.

Here are Jacqueline's final words on this topic…

Our culture unleashes many forms of toxic social programming, but few lessons seem to have as much impact as teaching girls the structure of the male ego. From the time I was in my mom's arms, I was epigenetically[13] influenced by the 'wisdom' passed on by my female ancestors. They engraved their beliefs into my tender brain: that I should flatter a man's sexual prowess and never say the truth of my intimate desires. The message was, sharing my intimate desires might be bothersome and may cause a man to be uncomfortable or see himself as imperfect.

Even ballsy, professional women, when in the bedroom, are reluctant to say, *"Please do it like this..."* or *"Would you please be gentler and slow down?"* Inherently, women know the consequences of confronting a man about his sexual prowess. This uncomfortable scenario instills passivity into our subconscious, making us believe that we're failures as women if we don't accept what's being done to our bodies. Then, when we don't achieve orgasm, men feel like failures. That's because they thought they were pleasing you the 'right way,' which is nothing more than a reflection of man's need for accomplishment. According to the Sexual Operating System, men must pleasure their female partner adequately to fend off competition. If that fails to happen, then a man questions his self-worth.

What a conundrum we humans find ourselves in, all because nature programs us to pursue our most primal instincts.

---

13 Recent research has shown that epigenetic influence extends beyond environmental genetic modification. It also involves the encoding of ancestral experiences, behaviors and beliefs from previous generations, resulting in potentially significant impacts on personality. http://discovermagazine.com/2013/may/13-grandmas-experiences-leave-epigenetic-mark-on-your-genes

Chapter 30

UPGRADE YOUR S.O.S. TO ACHIEVE EXTRAORDINARY SEXUAL INTIMACY

Our survival instinct is destroying us

The survival instinct is the foundation of Maslow's Hierarchy of Needs[14].

Maslow's Hierarchy of Needs*

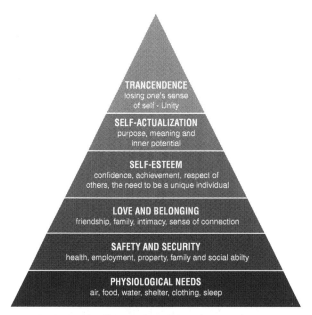

*authors added Transcendence as the highest level need

---

14 Maslow's Hierarchy of Needs is a theory in psychology proposed by Abraham Maslow in his 1943 paper *A Theory of Human Motivation* that essentially states that most individuals cannot focus on attaining higher level needs until their lower-level ones are first met.

Survival is the most powerful of our needs. Mostly, we have survived, individually and collectively, in terms of the propagation of our species. Unfortunately, this mostly unconscious drive is also the primary reason we have wars, greed, bigotry, intolerance, jealousy, suffering, torture and broken relationships.

If you peel away the layers of the onion for every one of these conditions, you will find at its core, the drive to survive. This drive is uncaring about how it fulfills its mission. If left unchecked, the same drive that brought us this far, is now threatening to tear us apart.

How the S.O.S. drives most relationships

Have you ever sensed an unseen force influencing your romantic relationships? Do you ever wonder why men check out other women when they already have one on their arm? For woman of childbearing years, do you wonder why the ticking of the biological clock can drive you insane, regardless of whether you desire children?

If so, you have glimpsed the default human Sexual Operating System (S.O.S.) at work. As revealed earlier, the S.O.S. provides crucial insight into the intricacies of human intimate behavior. But let's delve deeper.

The S.O.S. is a major component of our survival programming. That's because it drives the need for propagation of the species, which reflects *collective* rather than individual survival. We already established that our S.O.S. manifests differently within each gender because of their respective procreative roles. The way nature wired most men is to inseminate often and non-monogamously, which helps with species' growth and diversity. Men's almost uncontrollable urge for release when aroused is evidence of this drive's power. It is also the reason many men find other women attractive, even when they are in a committed, loving relationship.

The male drive for dominance is a result of this wiring too. This explains why so many males pursue the most attractive females. Success here is evident in their de facto superiority over other competing males.

In addition, nature wires men to provide so homo sapiens can propagate. This makes men goal-driven, action-oriented and less likely to relate with their true feelings. Our early ancestor likely equated displays of male emotional vulnerability with weakness and therefore undesirable in terms of tribal survival.

Likewise, the default S.O.S. wires most women to be nurturing and emotionally available to help their young assimilate into a dangerous and hostile world. It also drives women to attract a suitable mate to provide food, shelter, clothing and protection, while they focus on the children. Women who are self-sufficient can find this aspect of the drive quite irritating.

Orgasmic transcendence

As you can see, the default S.O.S. has a powerful influence over our relationship behaviors. So, if nature wired us this way, why so many unhappy couples? This is due to our evolved need for *self-actualization* and *transcendence*, found at the top of the hierarchy of needs. It is where these two opposing needs, survival instinct vs. conscious self-actualization/transcendence, are at odds.

For most couples, orgasm is their only experience with true transcendence. In this context, transcendence refers to the fleeting moments during climax when our survival-obsessed ego dissolves into a fearless and sublime unity with whom we shared the experience. We contend that the default S.O.S. stymies our ability to achieve and grow intimate transcendence.

Upgrade your Sexual Operating System

What we share with you below is what Jacqueline and I did to upgrade our respective S.O.S. This upgrade helped us achieve levels of emotional, sexual and spiritual intimacy beyond what most people consider possible.

PLEASE NOTE: What we share below consistently works for us. We don't assume the following steps are 'the way' for every couple to achieve extraordinary sexual intimacy. Jacqueline and I share them as inspiration for your unique journey to enhanced sexual intimacy we believe is available to everyone:

- ♡ **Truly listen** – Jacqueline is not shy about telling me what she wants in the bedroom. Thankfully, I've learned to listen and provide accordingly.

- ♡ **Vulnerability** – removing the barriers to one's Heart and allowing oneself to feel everything. This one goes so against the grain of the default S.O.S. that it can be difficult at first to adopt. However, the success of your S.O.S. upgrade and the quality of your relationship depends upon it.

- ♡ **Authenticity** – showing up as we are; it includes sharing our authentic thoughts and feelings in a vulnerable way without pretense, sarcasm or dissimulation.

- ♡ **Choose Presence over performance** – Presence is crucial when giving and receiving during sexual intimacy. This means no distractions, goals or agendas other than being present. Ironically, this upgrade alone results in experiences that exceed any performance couples previously had.

- ♡ **Embrace uncertainty** – view your relationship as a great adventure, one filled with unexpected surprises and gifts. Any real adventure includes uncertainty, which, when embraced, is the gateway to real relationship gold.

The above are the non-gender-specific S.O.S. upgrades. Now let's explore recommended upgrades for men and women.

Male-specific S.O.S. upgrades

Slow down to give your woman plenty of time for arousal. Notice how this approach is the exact opposite to the common default male S.O.S. response of: *"I've got a hard-on, let's go!"*

For males with E.D., your S.O.S. upgrade has a head start. Losing the urgency concomitant with an erection makes it easier to accommodate your partner's intimate desires. If you do not have E.D. and can get hard just thinking about a woman, we suggest that you masturbate before sexual intimacy. This is the recommended pre-intimacy preparation until you can control erectile urges and be sexually intimate in a state of Presence. When I mentioned this during an interview with a 30-something talk show host of a major broadcast radio show, he remarked, *"What!? I'd just fall asleep."* So much for cuddling after coitus.

Once you experience the extraordinary difference in sexual intimacy outcome, you can go back to allowing an erection at the start. This assumes you continue to exercise the restraint necessary to achieve these heightened results.

Female-specific S.O.S. upgrades

Jacqueline accepts and understands her body, and continually explores her sensual possibilities. Sadly, most women fail to achieve their full sexual potential due to religious and cultural influences. Based upon our limited observations, we believe most women can unlock their unlimited sensual potential at any age. This requires however, embracing their bodies and sexual energy without reservation.

As you might expect, Jacqueline has her 2-cents as well...

> Ladies, please listen carefully. The quickest way to upgrade your S.O.S. is to embrace, understand and love your sexuality and sensual potential. If you need outside coaching for this, or therapy to address previous sexual aggressions, seek it out *now*. Then find the courage to speak your truth about your newly discovered sexual wants and needs. Insist on it. Only when these conditions are in place will you and your partner have a chance to experience the profound sexual intimacy you each deserve.

Life beyond motherhood

Though rarely discussed, women need a sense of purpose and mission beyond motherhood. Apart from what you may believe, this need for purpose is not just a male trait, it's a human one. For many women, having and raising children *is* their #1 mission in life. What happens when they leave the nest? At that point, it will be just you, your partner and the surrounding four walls that beg the question: *"What now?"* If you haven't figured out your mission or purpose beyond the kids, it can create a dilemma that negatively impacts your relationship and life.

Some women, like me, see beyond the urge to bring children into this world. I personally would rather live a life teaching those already here to achieve self-actualization, higher consciousness and an upgraded S.O.S.

This is important to me because I am acutely aware that in a few decades, no one will remember my existence. From an evolutionary standpoint, my absence from the gene pool is a failure. How can I transcend this fate?

In my thirties, I asked myself this sobering question: Is finding a mate, making babies and living in the U.S. all there is to my life?

I read many books that showed me that there's more to life beyond being a mother. These wisdom-filled works were like islands in a sea of evidence to the contrary. On the other hand, my sister's and brother's genes survived, and will likely reproduce through subsequent generations. Through their children, they'll cheat death.

I want my legacy to be that all young women experience life a little longer before they choose whether to settle or not. Hopefully, they will wait to decide if having children is right for them. After a few generations of genetic mixing and shuffling, there's a possibility for a new generation of women to find another meaning in life: one born from consciousness and self-realization. That's what I subscribe to.

I upgraded my Sexual Operating System through living a conscious life that transcends ephemeral existence. Becoming self-aware and teaching other people to reach their greatest potential, in my mind, is a useful alternative to the traditional survival-based template life gave us.

Conscious vs. instinctive lovemaking

We define conscious lovemaking as a sexually intimate encounter where both parties have experienced an S.O.S. upgrade. Alternatively, we define instinctive lovemaking as intimate encounters driven by the procreative urge (whether having progeny is the intention or not). In the context of intimate behavior, 'conscious' means being aware and present, and 'unconscious' means instinctual and visceral. The remaining part of this chapter will refer to the conscious version of lovemaking.

Pleasuring each other

When you are both present, warmed up and (by now), quite turned-on, the rest of your sexual adventure awaits you. Here's a few thoughts to help you get the most out of your heightened lovemaking.

Once again, we turn to the book *She Comes First – The Thinking Man's Guide to Pleasuring a Woman* by Ian Kerner, Ph.D. It is an excellent reference for any man willing to learn how to ravish his woman via cunnilingus. The clitoris is a complex female organ whose sole purpose is pleasure. Despite its diminutive size, it has more nerve endings than the penis.

Jacqueline and I both immensely enjoy oral stimulation, which means, unlike intercourse, we never get tired, no matter how long we do it. As per my 'ladies first' rule, I first give pleasure to Jacqueline while maintaining a state of Presence. Then I slowly and gently massage her clitoris and surrounding genital area with my tongue and lips. This includes 'listening' to her body as my guide to giving her maximum pleasure without over-stimulation. We discovered that slight variations in the way my tongue touches different parts of her clitoris and its surrounding area can cause her to have an astonishing variety of orgasms. Any attempt on my part to explain her range of climatic experiences will inevitably fall short, so I'll leave that task to Jacqueline…

> My current experience is different in that the multiple orgasms of which Michael speaks have more power than any I previously experienced. I suspect the difference in my level of enjoyment is an 'inside job.' Becoming a more conscious person has paved the way for me to be present for Michael. In turn, he senses I'm available emotionally and physically to enjoy his affections and the vastness of my female sensuality.
>
> Each orgasm is different and ineffable. In an attempt to describe them, I would say the first orgasm is the doorway to as many as I'm open to receiving in any particular session. In my case, it often depends on whether my leg muscles fall into the not-so-sexy state of cramping. Each orgasm provides different sensations in different parts of my body. The first climax is usually the most powerful. However, subsequent orgasms, although typically smaller, bring experiences which are as pleasurable as they are different. I credit this wonderful full-body release to the work I do as a sexual being, by staying present while receiving this transcendent gift.

Ramp up

> Sometimes I must resort to a fantasy, focusing on something I find arousing. Once it takes root, I *know* I will climax. Now, let's talk about building up the tension to experience the release. As I sense the very start of my peak, I attempt to hold and drag it out for as long as possible. You will find this act alone is quite pleasurable. Then it reaches the point where I can't take it

anymore, and the explosion occurs with every fiber of my body tingling with pure ecstasy and aliveness.

I don't possess any special abilities over other women. Michael and I believe *all* women have this innate capability for unlimited sexual expression. It requires truly knowing and loving your sexual self, and having a coachable partner to 'create the space' to achieve your sexual potential.

When I sense Jacqueline is approaching climax, I ignore my innate urge to go harder and faster unless she indicates otherwise. This impulse is common in men because it works for us as we approach climax. Yet, our mutual reward for incorporating this discipline is beyond measure.

Giving permission

Now, here's a powerful insight we both learned about the female psyche that has a tremendous impact on our lovemaking. Sometimes Jacqueline has trouble reaching climax when she desires it. Typically, this happens because she is trying too hard, or her mind is still not fully present, despite our warm-up. This may be due to women's tendency for mental multitasking. When this happens, I stop, look up at her and ask: *"Sweetie, are you enjoying this?"* to which she consistently replies: *"OMG yes! But I don't think I can climax this time."* Then I respond with: *"That's okay, don't even try. I love doing this for you and I'm not the least bit tired. Just relax and enjoy it."*

By giving her 'permission' to not try anymore, she relaxes to receive my loving and almost always explosively climaxes 20 seconds later. Once that happens, the damn bursts, releasing a veritable flood of multiple orgasms that continue until she either develops leg cramps or wants to reciprocate. The point is, women have performance anxiety too, perhaps more than men. By giving your woman space to receive without expectation, you open the door to greater and more consistent peak sexual experiences.

Men, learn to receive

Men tend to give by doing. It's part of our DNA that wires us to protect and provide for our 'brood.' When translated to the bedroom however, this 'doing' is not always desirable. An important lesson I learned as an impotent male is that *trying* to achieve climax rarely works. I eventually surrendered to just receiving from Jacqueline as she performs fellatio on me. Just being present to how her tongue, lips and mouth felt on my penis, allowed my brain to spontaneously re-wire to experience orgasms of incredible power and duration. As mentioned earlier in the book, these climaxes are far beyond anything I ever imagined possible before cancer.

Once it became clear my prostate cancer was progressing, it was crucial to remove its 'fuel'—testosterone. The very idea of chemical castration therapy sent me into a tailspin. I was familiar with the side effects. The one I was most concerned with was losing my libido. I thought that meant saying goodbye, perhaps forever, to my drive to make love to Jacqueline, as well as those new powerful male orgasms I was so enjoying.

Here's what happened. I did lose my interest in sexual release, yet my desire to please Jacqueline continues unabated. That's because my greatest sexual fulfillment is giving her pleasure in the way she wants. However, this didn't stop Jacqueline from giving me incredible pleasure in the usual way during lovemaking.

With no testosterone in my system, I initially found it impossible to climax for the first few months under this new therapy. At one point, I thought I'd never experience an orgasm again. One day I stopped trying and relaxed into passively receiving from her without any expectations. Without warning, I had an orgasm so powerful I wept out of pure ecstasy and joy. It was so incredibly beautiful.

Consider *carefully* what I shared here. For the men reading this who are dealing with the challenges of cancer-induced impotence and castration therapy, this possibility is earthshaking (no pun intended). It means that, despite otherwise debilitating circumstances, you still have the possibility to enjoy levels of sexual release that may exceed what you experienced prior to your cancer. To do so requires letting go of trying, and *surrendering* to the sensual giving of your partner (someone hopefully well coached on what works for you).

It's not about the orgasm

One thing to remember is that making love consciously and in a state of Presence means being in the moment for each other whether giving or receiving. This includes no expectations whatsoever of the outcome. Counterintuitively, approaching your lovemaking this way will increase the possibility of you both achieving extraordinary climaxes and the female partner experiencing multiple and varied orgasms.

Sometimes Jacqueline and I make love when we choose *not* to climax, and instead enjoy a prolonged state of high sexual arousal. We find this to be yet another facet of our overall sexual intimacy—and just as satisfying as if we both had explosive releases.

A world of sensual possibilities

Dr. Kerner's book, mentioned earlier, is an excellent reference and starting point for both of you to explore the vast world of oral sex that can transform your relationship.

We understand oral pleasuring is not everyone's cup of tea. Obviously, many ways exist for enjoying sexual intimacy. Endeavor to discover them together as part of your journey to mutual sexual bliss. However, we have found the tongue to be a source of intense and prolonged pleasure. The tongue never tires and offers fine and subtle stimulation not available by any other means.

Should you pleasure your partner in this way, there are several caveats to keep in mind. First, avoid the 'Captain Crunch & Munch' syndrome. Slow and gentle is the preference for most women, even during climax. Also, should your partner reach orgasm and she is not too sensitive afterwards, *don't stop…* keep going gently and slowly. You may find she will eventually experience multiple orgasms. Don't stop until she says so or expresses an urgent desire to reciprocate. When it's the woman's turn to pleasure her man, he will benefit most from her gift by being present. Mastering the ability to receive passively in a state of Presence can open new sensual worlds for the male partner.

If you intend to follow what we outlined above, we hope you're ready for the most incredible sexual experience of your lives. This is the start of something beautiful for you and your partner: the ultimate sexual adventure cancer cannot touch.

SECTION 4

Exploring Spiritual Intimacy

"I, you, he, she, we. In the garden of mystic lovers these are not true distinctions."

~ RUMI

We are truly amazing creatures. Each of us can transcend the worst circumstances and innate survival instincts to connect with others. Yet, our capacity for intimate expression is so much more.

You have already seen how emotional intimacy is the foundation for deep, fulfilling sexual intimacy that can reach considerable heights. If you think of Heart-centered connection as emotional or sexual 'energy' that flows between two people, it opens the possibility of another form of energy. We call this 'Spiritual Intimacy,' which has no religious connotations. Spiritual Intimacy is equivalent to sexual life force[15], which everyone, with practice, can feel and exchange, but which current scientific methodologies cannot yet measure.

This last section is all about exploring Spiritual Intimacy as another powerful way to grow and experience deeply connecting intimacy with your partner. For many readers, this section will be an exciting eye-opener. For others, it may challenge entrenched cultural and religious beliefs, or even what it means to be male or female. We include these final chapters, not to change anyone's beliefs or question their sexual identity, but to present insights and experiences that most people don't even know exist—insights that continue to enhance profoundly the depth and breadth of intimacy Jacqueline and I enjoy.

This section is also the shortest of this book—for good reason. We are still exploring what is possible within this 'space' (one that seems to have no limits). So, once again, we humbly invite you to suspend temporarily any preconceptions or judgments. Just allow your adventurous spirit to explore what we share here and see how it resonates.

---

15 'Sexual life force' may bring to mind, for some readers, the ancient practice of Tantric Sex. While some of the methods and experiences shared within this section are similar to those who practice Tantra, we take a much more secular and simple approach to understanding and experiencing the exchange of sexual life force energy between partners.

Chapter 31

THE KISS

Why people kiss

We are a firm believer that most intimate behavior has a survival imperative behind it somewhere. Here's an excerpt from a recent article[16] *Why Do People Kiss?* which lends support to our contention:

> *"Today, the most widely accepted theory of kissing is that humans do it because it helps us sniff out a quality mate. When our faces are close together, our pheromones 'talk'—exchanging biological information about whether or not two people will make strong offspring. Women, for example, subconsciously prefer the scent of men whose genes for certain immune system proteins are different from their own. This kind of match could yield offspring with stronger immune systems, and better chances for survival."*

Jacqueline couldn't agree more because she will tell you that the first thing that attracted her was my *biological* scent, not my cologne.

Most strikingly, in the book *She Comes First: The Thinking Man's Guide to Pleasuring a Woman*, author Ian Kerner, Ph.D. cites research showing direct nerve connections between parts of a woman's upper lip and her clitoris. Enough said.

According to pundits, there are *155 different* kisses. That's a lot of kisses to remember and master. We have found kissing is not about

---

16 http://www.livescience.com/32464-why-do-people-kiss.html

quantity, variety or time spent lip-locked. Instead, kissing is that ineffable exchange that happens when lips touch and can transport their owners to entirely new worlds—*every... single... time.*

Kissing experts

When it comes to kissing, you are the experts. The key is learning how to do it in a way that enhances your mutual bliss rather than ascribing to someone else's idea of the perfect kiss. So with this in mind, we share our kissing insights to help you explore this delicious form of human communication.

Instead of pondering different kisses, let's explore the different *reasons* for kissing. Here's a partial list of those lip-locking intentions we have compiled for life's major kissable moments:

♡ **The first kiss** – this kiss is an intimate rite of passage with someone new. During your first kiss, you are likely thinking, *"Am I going to do it right or will I come off as a doofus?"* Just for the record, I was a slow learner, but that first one gave me plenty of encouragement to keep trying. Even experienced kissers can stress over the first kiss with someone new, as it could signal the start or end of a blossoming romance. No pressure there.

♡ **The passionate kiss** – this one is the expression of lust between two very horny people. The intensity of these kisses (also known as sucking face), is a response to each partner's growing arousal. These typically occur in the bedroom (or any other semi-convenient/private location)—or in bars after the third beer.

♡ **The 'I am here for you' kiss** – this kiss shows support, tenderness and empathy during challenging times.

♡ **The 'peck'** – this kiss is for quick greetings or farewells and occurs most often when either partner is in a hurry or distracted. This brief lip contact barely qualifies as a kiss in our book. We include it here because of its prevalence in our culture. What should be the least practiced kiss sadly seems to be the default for most couples.

♡ **The 'World ceases to exist' kiss** – now we're talking! Despite how long Jacqueline and I have been together, kissing this way is still one of our favorite ways to connect. First, I become very present and look deeply into Jacqueline's eyes—essentially kissing her with my Soul. Then, I gently take hold of her head and tilt it to one side, as I ever-so-lightly brush my lips against hers while softly stroking her cheek with my thumb. As we continue to do this, time stops and awareness of our surroundings and daily troubles disappear.

As you might suspect, Jacqueline has her thoughts about this as well…

I consider kissing a mating ritual that doesn't require getting naked. This last kiss is the one that brings us spiritual Unity, where we feel our spirits melt into each other. It works for Michael and I every time. It's shared here, not as the way to do it, but rather as an invitation to discover your own 'World ceases to exist' kiss. We now avoid the Peck, and use this kiss as our default every time we greet or say goodbye to each other. That's apart from all the other occasions in which we choose to meld.

Painting your love with a kiss

Consider the act of kissing as a work of art, imperfect, yet always in refinement. If you haven't discovered your mutual 'World ceases to exist' kiss yet, keep at it (ideally, at every opportunity throughout the day). By practicing in the Moment, it will reveal itself, eventually.

Chapter 32

THE BREATH OF INTIMACY

Energy flow

Jacqueline and I had the opportunity to experience Reiki energy work. Reiki is the Japanese Buddhist practice of aligning the seven Chakras of the body to allow life force energy to flow unimpeded. When a skilled Reiki practitioner works on you, they can achieve this result without touching.

As 'New Age' as this may sound, we have found it works, *powerfully*. My first three Reiki sessions took place over a six week period. After the first session, I felt relaxed. The second session left me drained to the point that I needed rest before driving home. The third session triggered a pronounced pulsing vibration up and down my spine. A friend, familiar with Reiki, said I had experienced a partial Kundalini release. Reiki practitioners define 'Kundalini' as dormant feminine sexual energy at the base of everyone's spine (whether male or female). Once this energy wakes, it can have a substantial, even overwhelming physical effect. According to my friend, if I had experienced a full Kundalini, I would have ended up in the hospital, delirious. While I find this inexplicable, I know what I experienced.

Just breathe

This Reiki healer knew of my erectile dysfunction and suggested that Jacqueline and I explore another way of being intimate by synchronizing our breathing. As always, we were open to trying something different.

We did many things to prepare us for this spiritual intimacy exercise. First, we cleared our minds and entered a deep state of Presence (i.e. no distractions, agendas or monkey-mind chatter). Then, we sat across from each other without touching, or, more effectively, Jacqueline sat on my thighs with her legs wrapped around my waist. This position allowed us to be nose to nose and look deeply into each other's eyes during the practice, which seems to enhance the effect (see figure below).

Once in position, she had us imagine a small ball of glowing energy in the space between our faces. As Jacqueline slowly exhaled, I inhaled, sucking in her breath (again, imagined as a ball of energy). As I exhaled, we visualized this energy ball traveling down my vertebrae and out the base of my spine. Jacqueline then inhaled it up through the base of her spine. We continued to visualize that ball traveling up her vertebrae and out her mouth as she exhaled once again, completing one cycle. With each cycle we 'sensed' that glowing ball of energy growing larger.

As you continue, one or both of you may experience profound physical sensations due to energy buildup. If so, it means you are exchanging your respective sexual energies to the point of harmonic resonance. This means each cycle adds to the overall power of the energy being exchanged. Like any other vibrational system, harmonic resonance can build high levels of energy quickly. The surest way to dampen or diminish this effect is to lose focus or fall out of Presence.

The last time Jacqueline and I practiced this, it affected my entire body. Initial Goosebumps turned to full-body shaking. It was the most incredible sensation—unlike anything I had ever had. While we experienced this as being highly sensual, it was not sexual in any way.

The un-tantra

Some people with whom we shared this experience remark something like: "*Oh, you two are practicing Tantra sex.*" Tantra is the ancient art of enhancing and exchanging sexual energy between two people. Its practices are complex, unlike the easy and straightforward method shared above.

After becoming more proficient, Jacqueline and I attended a weekend Tantra workshop led by well-known experts. To our dismay, we were already attaining the intended results of the course with greater simplicity and less effort. When we tried the methods being taught, it put us so much into our heads that it inhibited us from achieving the same effect.

Regardless of what you call it, this breath work is an easy way for you to exchange something sublimely powerful and experience a quality of intimacy you may never have thought possible. The best part is that you can practice it regardless of circumstances or physical limitations due to cancer.

Chapter 33

EXPLORING INTIMATE BOUNDARIES

Human beings are restless creatures. We easily become bored and seek new experiences. Whether it means learning a new skill, traveling to new places, making scientific discoveries or colonizing Mars, we individually and collectively keep pushing boundaries. Variety is the motivating spice of a rich and fulfilling life, especially in the bedroom. No matter how attracted and turned-on you are for each other, sexual routine and boredom will take its toll. Frustration, wandering eyes and affairs are often the result. It doesn't need to be this way, nor must you settle for the 'same-ole, same-ole' in the sack.

Fortunately, a way exists to help prevent this from happening, one which reveals new sensual worlds and keeps things fresh and exciting for the full term of your relationship.

Half of our sexual potential

Jacqueline and I have a friend who has a deep understanding of sexuality and relationships. Although he is in his 70s, he is still quite sexually active and adventurous. He once mentioned how, in a recent relationship, his female partner playfully fondled his chest and nipples in the same way he did to her. To his surprise, he found it to be a source of new pleasure.

Upon hearing this, Jacqueline and I turned to each other with a knowing smile, because this experience is something we discovered on our own, years ago. He went on to say that if this happened during his younger years, he might have been uncomfortable with it.

So, what's going on here?

Well, several things. The first has to do with why men can experience arousal by having their nipples fondled. The second is about why this nipple tickle unsettles them?

Culturally acceptable (and constrained), intimate behaviors are the norm for most heterosexual couples. The male is usually dominant, and the female passive. Although this seems obvious, it has less to do with physicality than you might think. Masculine sexual energy tends toward dominant giving. Feminine sexual energy tends more towards passive receiving.

Now, if you stay open-minded, this is where things get interesting for new sensual possibilities. Think of sexual energy as a *continuum* within every human being, regardless of gender or orientation, as illustrated below:

Sexual Energy Continuum

The closer one is to either extreme of the continuum, the less of the opposite sexual energy they have. Most people fit within the interior of this continuum, and have elements of both masculine and feminine sexual energy. In most heterosexual couples, the male partner's position on the continuum is somewhere on the left side, and the female is on the right.

When Jacqueline and I place ourselves on the sexual energy continuum, we find ourselves near the center. That's because I have a strong feminine sexual energy component, and Jacqueline has a strong masculine one. Most importantly however, we use these opposite energies to *double* our pleasure.

Let's consider the possibility that *how fully one expresses their sexual energy determines the quality of their intimate experience.* This means, the more you allow yourself to express the full spectrum of your sexual energy, the more powerful and fulfilling your experience can be.

Gender energy swapping

Most couples' sexual intimacy run on four cylinders when they have a supercharged V-8 under the hood, just aching to unleash its sensual power. When we coach couples about achieving extraordinary intimacy, we show them how to express their sexual energy beyond any inherent binary bias. We do this by encouraging spontaneous shifting back and forth of their masculine and feminine energy expression during lovemaking sessions. This is a process we call 'gender energy swapping.'

For men, this includes allowing themselves to surrender totally, and *passively* receive their partner's giving. For women, this means giving to their partner in a more dominant way and feeling the sense of power that emerges. Just to be clear, we are *not* referring to BDSM[17], only a willingness to experience and express the full spectrum of sexual energy. Based on our limited observations, heterosexual men, far more than straight women, are reticent about allowing their opposite gender sexual energy to emerge in any form. Perhaps they consider it a sign of weakness or latent homosexuality.

I see my feminine side as one of my biggest strengths as a man. It balances out my more aggressive, masculine side. It also allows me to enjoy more subtle and nuanced sensual experiences, especially in the context of being impotent due to cancer. However, while I appreciate the beauty of the male form, it holds no sexual interest for me at all.

---

17 BDSM is a variety of often erotic practices or role playing involving bondage, discipline, dominance and submission, sadomasochism, and other interpersonal dynamics. See https://en.wikipedia.org/wiki/BDSM

Here are a few words of advice from Jacqueline for our female readers…

There's no room for 'playing safe' when planning a lovemaking adventure with a partner who is a cancer survivor. There are many ways and areas of his body to consider for intimate foreplay. One example is fondling your partner's nipples, as Michael mentioned. Ladies, respect his reaction to this new exploration. Some men love this; others will balk. If he does, don't take it personally, just playfully explore other places. Also, be aware that he may be shy about allowing his feminine side to show. Don't rush him, instead, always reassure him with your presence and total acceptance of him. Eventually, he will feel safe to play.

Assuming you are both comfortable allowing your opposite gender energies to emerge, the process of incorporating this into your lovemaking is quite straightforward.

Here's how it works for us

Like most lovers, we take turns being on top. This indicates which one of us is manifesting masculine energy. The one on bottom will be receiving, which, in this context, signals feminine energy. When Jacqueline is on top, I often imagine that I am receiving her thrusts as if she were the man. Similarly, she imagines herself being the man while thrusting into me.

When Jacqueline and I are in sync this way, through the lens of my erotic imagination, I can feel her penetrate me as she thrusts her hips into mine. It's as if I had a vagina, and she a penis. At the same time, Jacqueline imagines she has a penis that is penetrating me. Of course, no physical penetration is occurring. The *energetics* of those thoughts provide the experience.

We typically switch our gender energy at least a half-dozen times during lovemaking sessions. We think of it as a sacred dance where we each take turns fluidly leading and following, with no words necessary.

It is incredibly erotic, and greatly enhances the variety and quality of our lovemaking.

What is so intriguing about this approach is, once you allow your opposite energies to emerge, those dormant perspectives go beyond just imagination. You are sourcing another part of yourself that was always there.

Here is Jacqueline's unique perspective about gender sexual energy…

I'd like to introduce you to a term I started to use. 'Slash' denotes the gender infinite variation between male and female. It represents ways we define sexual identity. We derive this term based on how we associate two opposites in the English language (i.e. male/female). When Michael and I gender energy swap, my feminine/masculine sexual selves merge and take on a different role in my sexual pleasure, in terms of both giving and receiving. 'Slash' occurs without my mind getting in the way, labeling what I do and how I do it. 'Slash' does away with labels. When I am in this state, I'm channeling my desire to give and receive love beyond gender identification. When I am 'Slash,' I am simply a complete and infinitely variable sexual being.

Testosterone makes a difference

As a side note, the energetic penetration described above is also a way for us to leverage our default Sexual Operating System, which, by definition, is penetration-centric. One thing I have noticed is my testosterone levels seem to influence the urge for penetration, whether giving or receiving. As mentioned earlier, prior to the chemical castration that keeps my T-levels near zero, my natural testosterone was off the charts.

At one point, it reached 1,327, where the normal high reference range for men is just over 800. At those levels, I had a pronounced urge for penetration. Now, with my lower levels, that has faded away. However, I still enjoy passively receiving whatever Jacqueline wishes to give me, whenever she feels like expressing more of her masculine side.

Typically, Jacqueline takes the lead in directing our energetic assignments. That is because my masculine energy can sometimes be too intense for her in the initial stages of our lovemaking. Regardless, it has become a mutually intuitive exchange, where we just know what to do without having to say a word.

Gender empathy

Something else happens for Jacqueline and I when we allow this immense freedom of expression to take place. We become more aware of the experience of 'being' the opposite gender. This provides us a context in which to appreciate each other, in and out of the bedroom.

If you are a man, we encourage you to explore allowing your full feminine side to emerge. This means passively receiving while being present, without expectations, goals, or especially self-judgment. Likewise, if you are a woman, wait until you see how excited your partner can become when you assert your masculine energy.

Unfortunately, many heterosexual couples may resist exploring this expanded world of sexual intimacy. This may be because men, especially in their mid-30s and older, seem to resist their innate feminine side due to concerns of being labeled a latent homosexual. Anecdotally, we also noticed that men in their 60s or older may be more open to it. This is perhaps due to age-related increasing levels of estrogen in their systems[18]. Likewise, we suspect that Millennial men are not as uptight about expressing their feminine side, given their generation's well-studied acceptance of gender identification fluidity[19].

In case you had any doubts, straight men can express and enjoy their feminine sexual energy without losing their sense of being a heterosexual male. Any concerns or fears to the contrary are mostly due to limiting beliefs thanks to cultural and religious bias—beliefs that can shift, with courage and an adventurous spirit.

18 http://universityhealthnews.com/daily/nutrition/8-surprising-high-estrogen-symptoms-in-men

19 http://www.npr.org/2014/11/30/363345372/for-these-millennials-gender-norms-have-gone-out-of-style

Looking elsewhere

One of the first temptations for a couple experiencing sexual routine is for one or both of the people involved to seek new sexual partners. This almost always damages the existing relationship, even if both partners consent. This strategy can never fill the hole of sexual dissatisfaction, it will only make it larger. Nor will it give the one who wanders a fraction of the experience they can have by allowing for the full mutual expression of their integrated masculine/feminine sexual energy. Most of us are not used to allowing our opposite sexual energy to express itself. Just know that when you surrender to it, you open yourself to endless sexual adventure and variety: a journey that never gets old, and takes you to sensual levels beyond anything you have experienced before.

Here's Jacqueline on how my cancer has been a blessing to our intimacy in a way that will never grow stale...

> Being Michael's life partner has been a beautiful and humbling experience. As a first-time partner of a cancer survivor, I cannot tell you how much our circumstances have taught us about our capacity to love and be truly intimate with each other. After diagnosis, cancer forces survivors to plunge into a 'new normal' of sexual functioning, and courageously address this important part of their lives.
>
> When we are sitting in our 'new normal,' it often surprises us to find that doing something different is good for the soul. In fact, as this whole book has been saying, we have discovered enormous changes in our outlook and our behavior that are incredible. It has been our miracle. Cancer will make you rethink your behavioral patterns in and out of the bedroom. Cancer invites you to learn a new way of living, and to think and connect in the ways that really matter.

Last words of encouragement.

We are truly amazing, conscious creatures with a limitless capacity for profound human connection—a connection that neither cancer, nor the impact of its treatment, could ever prevent you from sharing.

Don't let limiting beliefs or fear of the unknown and unfamiliar stop you from enjoying life's most precious gift—a sacred intimacy with your life partner that transcends time, space and circumstances.

Your adventure to the land of extraordinary intimacy has just begun.

Epilogue

A woman is not a light switch; she is more like a volume knob. Women rarely experience the same progression of excitement, plateau, orgasm and resolution as men, but that doesn't mean they have less libido. They just have more sensual variety.

Scientists still do not understand how female arousal works, or what triggers it. While we wait, my message to all women is this: you no longer have to fit anyone else's notion of what it means to be sexual… all you have to do is become aware of your unique sensual potential.

There will be times when you feel your relationship has lost the sense of mystery and risk you experienced before domesticity and autopilot kicked-in. Michael and I avoid this by challenging each other with little creative and playful endeavors. That's a turn on for me because it's as if I'm not having sex with the same person all the time.

Ask yourself, what is the most important thing in your life. Most people would agree it's their intimate relationship. Consider that every other important aspect of our life demands we learn about it: whether it's our career, parenting skills, sports, et cetera… The only thing humans leave to chance is their relationships. This results in an unhappy, unstable emotional life. Crazily, we often repeat the same behaviors when we find someone new. Are we really expecting different results by doing the same things repeatedly?

True intimacy requires slow motion in everything we do, as well as being fully present. I am asking you to enjoy every second of the ride. Time waits for no one, especially for those we love with cancer. Remember, intimacy is a journey, not a destination. Women, use your innate communication skills. Men, ask what your partner wants, be a good listener and be willing to handle positive or negative feedback. These truths are not only important, they're everything.

About the Authors

"The best way to find yourself is to lose yourself in the service of others."

~ Mahatma Gandhi

Michael J. Russer is an international speaker, TEDx alum, author and thought leader who is clinically impotent because of prostate cancer. It is because of his impotence he and his life partner and co-author, Jacqueline Lopez, discovered an entirely new approach to experiencing levels of emotional, sexual and spiritual intimacy. Their deep analysis of how his impotence 're-wired' their approach to and experience of intimacy led to their advanced Sexual Operating System model of human intimate behavior.

Earlier in his career, he was a programmer/systems analyst, as well as an international technology speaker and adult education curriculum developer for nearly 20 years. This background, along with his extensive experience with transformational pedagogical methodologies enabled him, and Jacqueline, to codify their own relationship experience into the real-world, reproducible approach to sex and intimacy found in this book.

Jacqueline V. Lopez is a native of Brazil and Paraguay. Her rich cultural heritage enables her to bring a very empowering and uninhibited feminine perspective to this work. This is crucial given that most Western societies tend to be repressed and uninformed about female sexuality. Her absolute authenticity and integrity was the fertile soil that allowed the transformative discoveries shared in this book to fully blossom.

As a professional speaker, she and Michael speak together to cancer survivors and their partners (often pro-bono), all over North America. She also speaks to menopausal women on how menopause can be the threshold to the greatest and most fulfilling intimacy of their lives.

She is a radio host, Certified Public Accountant, CEO of a Web Development firm and TEDx organizer. In addition to single-handedly organizing, launching and selling out the Chumash TEDx event in San Luis Obispo, CA, she founded the Santa Barbara Chapter of the American Wine Society and the Central Coast Women's Network.

Jacqueline is passionate about helping everyone actualize their highest possibilities, whether within their intimate relationship or as human beings making a difference in the world.

It is Michael's and Jacqueline's mission in life to empower all people, regardless of race, creed or orientation, single or in relationship, to achieve deeply connecting Heart-centered intimacy in the face of cancer, or any other of life's challenges.

Additional Resources

No original body of work comes without help—it always stands on the shoulders of others who have come before. Besides our own personal experiences, discoveries and ongoing journey with cancer and intimacy, Jacqueline and I have been deeply influenced and helped by most of the resources shared below. There are others we included here that we feel could be of benefit as you navigate the travails associated with cancer and its impact on your experience of all forms of intimacy.

We hope you find these to be as beneficial as we have.

Recommended Books

♡ *The Presence Process: A Journey Into Present Moment Awareness* (by Michael Brown) – this book has had an enormous impact on our ability to achieve and maintain being fully present for each other, which is crucial for all forms of ongoing intimacy.

♡ *Stillness Speaks* (by Eckhart Tolle) – this book, more than any other, has influenced our thinking about the duality of ego vs. the Heart, which resulted in the extremely empowering context found throughout the book you now hold in your hands. *(NOTE: Michael has read this book cover-to-cover dozens of times, and uses it as a source of inspiration nearly every day.)*

♡ *The Power of Now* (by Eckhart Tolle) – a work we found to be very helpful in our ability to live fully Aware in the Moment.

- ♡ *She Comes First: The Thinking Man's Guide to Pleasuring a Woman* (by Ian Kerner, Ph.D.) – an excellent, well-written and entertaining guide for any man (or woman), who is interested in pleasing their female partner in the most effective way possible. *One word of caution:* Don't assume the techniques shared will work for your partner. This book is fine to use as a source of mutual sensual inspiration, however, your partner is always the final arbiter of what works best for her.

- ♡ *Come as You Are* (by Emily Nagoski, Ph.D.) – a superb resource for any woman who wants help becoming comfortable with their body and full sensual potential (something many women in our Western culture continue to struggle with today).

- ♡ *The Disposable Male: Sex, Love, and Money, Your World through Darwin's Eyes* (by Michael Gilbert) – this book provides a well-researched evolutionary anthropological perspective on why men and women are the way they are, and the underlying forces that powerfully influence many aspects of committed relationships.

- ♡ *How Two: Have a Successful Relationship* (by Phil and Maude Mayes) – a wonderful, practical book by two septuagenarians with an incredible relationship who, for the betterment of all, have decided to share their relationship success secrets.

Support Organizations

The support organizations listed below represent just a small portion of what is available to cancer survivors and their partners, typically at no charge. We show them here because we worked with them directly, or they are familiar to us, because of our own journey dealing with cancer.

- ♡ **Cancer Support Community** – our favorite non-profit support organization for all cancer survivors and their partners. It has centers all over North America and a few overseas. It costs nothing to be a member and the support these

dedicated folks offer is nothing short of amazing.
(http://cancersupportcommunity.org)

♡ **Susan G. Komen** – probably the best known non-profit support group for breast cancer survivors.
(http://ww5.komen.org/BreastCancer/Support.html)

♡ **BreastCancer.org** – another non-profit support organization dedicated to breast cancer survivors.
(http://breastcancer.org)

♡ **Prostate Cancer Education Council** – this non-profit organization dedicates its efforts to educating all men, and their partners, on the detection, treatment, and life impact of prostate cancer. We've worked with this group directly, and they are wonderful, dedicated and very competent people.
(http://prostateconditions.org)

♡ **US TOO** – another non-profit resource designed to help all men and their partners deal with all aspects of prostate cancer.
(http://ustoo.org)

Miscellaneous Resources

The following resources are from third-parties, or from Jacqueline and I, in effort to help cancer survivors and their partners achieve high levels of intimacy in the face of cancer.

♡ **The ManKind Project New Warrior Training Adventure (NWTA)** – the transformational three-day intensive workshop I mentioned in Chapter 2. I highly recommend this for men of all ages, regardless of circumstances.
(http://mankindproject.org)

♡ **Cancer Intimacy Help** – this website is designed to help all cancer survivors achieve deep intimacy and fulfillment in the face of cancer. It also provides an opportunity

for couples to request private coaching with us.
(http://CancerIntimacyHelp.com)

♡ **MasterHeart Template** – here you can download a Word doc template to help facilitate your own MasterHeart meetings. (http://CancerIntimacyHelp.com/resources)

♡ **SOS Insight** – this website allows couples (whether affected by cancer or not) to participate in the three-day transformational intimacy workshops we offer in major cities around the world. The basis of this powerful program is our advanced Sexual Operating System (S.O.S.) model of human intimate behavior. Prospective participants must go through a rigorous application process before being accepted into the program. (http://SOSInsight.com)

♡ **Menopausal Women** – this is a great resource for menopausal women to find their way back to deeply fulfilling emotional and sexual intimacy. (http://JacquelineVLopez.com)

Reaching out

Jacqueline and I invite you to reach out to us at any time with questions or comments. You can email us at contact@sosinstitute.org, or call us at 805-699-5504.

Acknowledgments

We never would have started or completed this book without the help, advice and support from many individuals. We are incredibly indebted to our dear friend and mentor, Michael Gilbert, who is the author of *The Disposable Male: Sex, Love, and Money, Your World through Darwin's Eyes*. Michael encouraged us to take the 100+ articles on sex, intimacy and relationships we wrote over the previous three years, and condense them down to an accessible and hopefully healing tome. He saw that we had something unique to contribute to this important aspect of being human, and insisted that we share it with the world.

We owe an incalculable debt of gratitude to our tireless, devoted and extremely talented developmental editor and writing mentor Kim Green in Atlanta, GA (Words, LLC). The first draft of this book was chaotic, as our passion had taken us in many directions. Her efforts organized this book to where it was finally worthy of reader's time and attention. She is a rare jewel of an editor and human being who saw the promise of our work within the disarray of the initial manuscript.

Likewise, we so appreciate the efforts of our copy editor, Mitchell Bogatz, who provided invaluable scrutiny and feedback to help make this book as polished as possible.

We were also fortunate to have several very talented individuals in their respective fields of expertise review the first draft of the book, each from their own unique perspective. Dr. Julie Taguchi, an oncologist and speaker to women about sex after breast cancer, provided invaluable candid feedback and encouragement. This helped us frame the book for survivors and partners of all types of cancer. Sean Hebbel, Program Director for the Cancer Support Community in Delaware, provided critical feedback to ensure the material within these pages was very much on track. He also provided suggestions on how to make it even more valuable to the people he and his staff serve every day. Encouragement and feedback from his CEO, Nichole Pickles, also made it easier to devote the untold hours needed to refine this book so it has the greatest chance of helping others. We hold deep gratitude for both.

We owe many thanks to Duncan Teague and David Thurman. Besides incisive, in-depth suggestions and critiques, they also helped us tailor our material in a way that LGBTQIA readers can find relevant value in what we shared.

A special thank you for our dear friend and advisor, Dr. Mitra Goosheh, PhD. Her gentle spirit introduced to us the incredible healing possibilities of Reiki energy work. She also guided us to our first experience of spiritual intimacy through synchronized breathing, which formed the foundation for the fourth section of this book.

Through a series of incidents, we met our friends, Phil and Maude Mayes, who are experts in maintaining successful relationships. We feel humble gratitude for knowing them, and for receiving the wisdom that they shared so freely with us. Strangely enough, we met our mentor, Michael Gilbert, at Maude's birthday party. If it weren't for that, our book may never have happened.

To all the incredibly dedicated people of the Cancer Support Community and Gilda's Clubs around the U.S., we say a big, *"Thank you!"* You were among the first cancer support groups that believed in our work, and provided so many speaking opportunities for us to share our message on stage with your members. You also work ceaselessly to help your members with all cancer-induced struggles. All of you are our inspiration, and the reason we provide a special electronic version of this book free to all your constituents.

To us, it's important that a book looks as good as it reads. We received many compliments on the cover and internal layout design of the book. This is all due to the wonderful creative talents of Justine

Elliott, owner of Lasso Design, who lives somewhere in beautiful New Zealand. We owe you many thanks for your inspired work.

I also want to acknowledge someone (who will remain nameless for many reasons), who served as the catalyst for me to remove the barriers I had so ardently put up in front of my Heart for most of my adult life. I believe I would be dead now if I hadn't taken the chance of becoming open-Hearted. What years of therapy of every kind failed to do, this person provided by simply pointing out the fact that I had shutdown. They then shoved me off the precipice of fear so I could learn to fly with my new wings of being Heart-open. My experience of life instantly transformed when it happened almost six years ago. For that, my gratitude is forever.

Along the same lines, I am so thankful to have found and become a proud member of The ManKind Project. This non-profit organization helps men worldwide embrace their full humanity and use it for the greater good of all. Thanks to their New Warrior Training Adventure program, my Heart is now open to the entire human species, not just to women. I believe if I hadn't gone through that transformation, it's likely that Jacqueline and I would never have made it as a couple, and this book wouldn't even exist.

Finally, Jacqueline and I are both very grateful for the one condition which many men fear more than death—my full clinical impotence. It is because of this circumstance and our full acceptance of it that you have this book in your hands. Whatever wisdom you derive from these pages started there. Our extraordinary relationship—that is more fulfilling every day—started there, and continues to flourish into new possibilities.

As strange as it may sound, my impotence has been, and continues to be, the biggest blessing to our relationship. It is the gift that is the gentle reminder of what constitutes genuine, deeply connecting intimacy. For that, we can never be thankful enough.

Made in the USA
San Bernardino, CA
05 November 2019

59419322R00111